RISOTTO! RISOTTO!

RISOTTO!

VALENTINA HARRIS
RISOTTO!

80 recipes and all the know-how you need to make Italy's famous rice dish

PHOTOGRAPHS BY MARTIN BRIGDALE

CASSELL

DEDICATION

To Phil Dodds. Dear Friend,
there is an author in there, I know there is.
Let him out!!

This edition first published in the UK 1998 by
Cassell
Wellington House
125 Strand
London WC2R 0BB

Text copyright © Valentina Harris 1998

Food photography © Martin Brigdale 1998

Photograph on page 17 AKG Photo, London
Photographs on pages 11, 12 and 14
Mary Evans Picture Library, London

British Library Cataloguing-in-Publication Data
A catalogue record for this book is available from
the British Library

ISBN 0-304-35010-9

Edited by Wendy Hobson
Designed and typeset by Harry Green
Food styling by Helen Trent
Home economist Maxine Clark
Assistant to home economist Julie Beresford
Printed and bound in Italy by New Interlitho

Contents

ACKNOWLEDGEMENTS

I would like to thank Deborah Taylor for the opportunity to write a book about one of my favourite things, and letting me do it my way! Thank you also to Martin and Helen, who always make everything I write look so beautiful, and to Maxine for cooking it just like I do. And a big thank you to Wendy for her patience and understanding on a very lovely book. May there be many more for us all.

I am deeply indebted to **Riso Gallo s.p.a.** of Robbio, Italy for all the fascinating material they have sent me and allowed me to use for my research on The History of Risotto and Types of Rice. My thanks also go to the team at **Gallo UK Ltd** for their kind help and support.

A huge thank you to Helen Hibbert at **ECM Housewares**, UK distributors for **Rondine**, for her support in providing a seemingly endless supply of fabulous cookware in which to cook and experiment with recipes at home. For information regarding where the pans are available, please call 01494 866006.

The author and publisher would also like to thank:
Carluccio's, Specialists in Italian Food and Funghi, 28a Neal Street, London WC2H 9PS (telephone 0171 240 5710; fax 0171 497 1361) for kindly lending the magnificently huge black and white truffles in the photograph on page 72.
Lina Stores, Italian Food Store, 18 Brewer Street, London W1 (telephone 0171 437 6482) for lending the beautiful prosciutto di Parma in the photograph on page 114.
Pauline Pears and Jackie Gear at **The Henry Doubleday Research Association**, Ryton Organic Gardens, Coventry CV8 3LG (telephone 01203 303517) for sacrificing personal beetroots for the photograph on page 46 and giving advice on cardoons.
Rona Hurcombe at **Divertimenti**, 139–141 Fulham Road, London SW3 6SD (telephone 0171 581 8065; fax 0171 823 9429) for lending the pans and other equipment used in the step-by-step guides to making stock and risotto on pages 24–25 and 34–35.

Rice is born in water,

but it must die in wine.

(Meaning, don't drink water

when eating risotto!)

Introduction

I am really pleased to have had the opportunity to write a whole book about one of my favourite Italian dishes: risotto. Risotto was the very first thing I ever learned to cook when I was about four years old and it is my earliest childhood memory. I can remember exactly the chair I stood upon and the feel of the gas ring heat near my legs, the way the wooden spoon felt in my hand and the intense perfume of the rice as it rippled and bubbled in the huge pot. Perhaps that was the moment I became hooked on cooking, and on risotto in particular.

Risotto is such a marvellous multi-purpose dish. It makes fantastic party food as it can easily be eaten with a fork whilst standing up; it is popular with children; can be as expensive and extravagant or as cheap and cheerful as you like; and is endlessly adaptable. As you can see from the recipes gathered together in this collection, there are very few ingredients which cannot be used to make a satisfying risotto.

The specifics for making risotto are very simple: you need the right kind of rice, the best possible stock (except for a few exceptions which use water or wine), the right width and depth of heavy-based pan, a favourite wooden spoon, a little patience and 20 minutes of stirring time.

You cannot hurry a good thing, and a risotto needs 20 minutes of being lovingly stirred to achieve success. In each recipe I have explained exactly how this happens, even though almost all risotti are cooked using the same basic technique. However, the common technique of toasting the rice grains then gradually adding the liquid is a relatively modern method. Risotto-making goes back much further than that, and in the old days the rice was cooked in a different way by boiling it with other ingredients. I have added a couple of those recipes because I believe they are interesting and because the finished dishes are delicious. I do hope you will enjoy the relaxed, soothing pastime of making risotto. It is an excellent way to wind down after a hard day and always a joy to eat.

Risotto should always be eaten with a fork from a soup plate or *fondina*. The risotto should be piled in a mound in the centre of the plate, then pulled outwards towards the edges of the plate, using the back of the prongs of the fork, a little at a time, mouthful by mouthful. Flattening the risotto on to the plate's surface with the back of the fork is permitted, as this not only helps you to get it safely on to your fork and up to your mouth but also aids the cooling process.

In Italy, risotto is served as a first course, or in a very few cases as a traditional accompaniment to a main course dish. For example, *Risotto alla Milanese* is often served with *Ossobucco*. In today's climate of smaller appetites, especially outside the boundaries of Italy, risotto will sometimes represent the main course, or even the entire meal, served with salad and fruit.

I hope that by the time you finish reading *Risotto! Risotto!* you'll be completely confident in tackling countless versions of this great Italian classic.

Buon risotto e buon appetito!

The History of Risotto

My journey of discovery to uncover the roots of this most wonderful dish has taken me quite literally from East to West. There was so much material, so much information to sift through until I could get a clear picture of the facts and the legend behind risotto, that there were times when I despaired of finding space in the book – I even thought we might have to cut out some of the recipes to make room! In the end, I reluctantly condensed everything into what I hope will be as fascinating for you to read as it was for me to research and write.

Rice is one of those foodstuffs which, over time, has set a tone and shaped the civilization of entire areas of our planet. In simple terms, the world can be divided into quarters and a basic grain assigned to each one: maize for the Americas, millet for Africa, wheat for the Mediterranean and rice for Asia.

Some historians tell us that the first archaeological evidence of rice, as both a wild and cultivated plant, go back as far as the first millennium BC. From those remote origins in China and other parts of the Orient, it would appear that rice made its way to southern India, and from there to Asia Minor, carried by nomads and traders. Although it was not until much later that it became linked with areas outside south-east Asia, it was, in fact, first seen by Alexander and his Greco-Macedonian troops in the fourth century BC, and a satirical tale written by Horace concerning a miser who complains bitterly to his doctor about the price of a rice tisane, tells us that it must have gained some medicinal usage.

As a crop, however, it did not have a wide impact either in Greece or the Mediterranean until the Arabs, with their great inventiveness and ability to bring their ancient wisdom to all manner of things including the kitchen, brought rice into the picture during the Middle Ages. Having introduced rice into Egypt and along the African coast, they then began to plant it both in Sicily and in Spain.

Rice-growing remained exclusive to those areas of the Mediterranean for some time, until eventually it was introduced into Lombardy and the rest of northern Italy. Gradually it became part of the familiar daily diet and lost its reputation as a remedy for sickness, although its usage as a curative must have continued to some degree, as records dated 1250 of the Dukes of Savoy show that rice was bought for the hospital of Sant'Andrea in Vercelli – a major rice-growing area – to make a special medicinal confection.

Elsewhere, rice – along with other items such as spices and sugar from far-flung places – was still considered to be an exotic ingredient. It was purchased

Flooding the fields in China before planting the rice, about 1850.

from the specialist shops of Genoese, Venetian and Arab merchants, who acquired it from as far away as their ships could sail, and sold it at ridiculously high prices. To give you some idea of its value during the course of its history, the Milanese tribunal of 1336 set a price of 12 Imperials per pound for rice, compared with a price of 8 Imperials a pound for honey.

Outside Spain and Sicily, the northern Italians and other Europeans were now beginning to use it as a ground grain, making it into rice flour with which they started to create recipes. The most famous of these is the ubiquitous *Bianco Mangiare* – now transmogrified into something pretty hideous as Blanc Mange in a sachet with dubious rice origins! – which, as the name suggests, was a dish made entirely from white ingredients: rice flour, goat or almond milk and white fish fillets or white poultry, all turned into a thick, creamy dish with a texture rather like a pudding, which could be sweet or savoury. Variations on this recipe appear in cookery books from various parts of Europe dating from the fourteenth and fifteenth centuries.

In the fifteenth century, rice began to take hold in other regions of Italy, in the areas which are now Tuscany, Piedmont and Lombardy, as well as in various other parts of northern Europe. Lombardy in particular was at the forefront of the

Cultivation of rice at Manila in the Philippines, about 1857.

development of rice cultivation in the flat, damp, fog-bound countryside that makes up great tracts of the region. Starting in the Milanese and Veronese provinces in 1390, rice cultivation spread to the Saluzzese provinces in 1465, then into Tuscany in the Pisa province in 1468. Further plantations were created in Milan in 1475 and in Vercelli in 1493.

It remains unclear as to whether rice originally made its way into Italy from the north or from Sicily and Spain. One link which might shed some light on the northern connection is the similarity between early Italian rice dishes and early Flemish recipes, dating back to a time when Lombardy and Flanders were both under the rule of King Charles V of Spain. In particular, what looks very much like a forerunner of *Risotto alla Milanese* appears in a famous painting by Pieter Brueghel of a peasant wedding. If indeed it is an early saffron risotto in those plates, this particular risotto is one of the oldest and most traditional. It crops up in many Lombard legends as a symbol of celebration, owing largely, I think, to its golden colour. It is often linked to marriage in many stories.

The other theory is that rice began to arrive in Spain and Portugal from 1498 to 1505 as a result of Spanish and Portuguese merchants travelling to Calcutta and Goa. Perhaps it was presented at and adopted by the Spanish court of Naples and made its way north to Lombardy and Piedmont with the Spanish troops of Frederick of Aragon.

Taking all the evidence into account, I like to think that both sources of influence – one from the north and one from the south – were relevant, because Italians eat rice in very different ways at either end of their country.

In the north, the habit of boiling up rice in broth or stock with other ingredients, as an early way of making risotto, led to the development of a fat, rounded, absorbent grain. In the south, on the other hand, a more Arabic-influenced cooking method prevails, whereby the rice is boiled first, then dressed with other ingredients to create a rice salad, for example. To this day, there is therefore less demand for absorbent risotto rice.

What is certain is that during the fifteenth century, rice cultivation, as opposed to rice as an exotic and expensive import, started to become part of life in the area of Lombardia called Lomellina. What's more, it was considered solely the property of the aristocracy and landed gentry of the Dukedom of Milan. Levies and taxes were imposed on all forms of export from the region, even into neighbouring areas.

Then, in 1475, we have evidence in two letters written by my own ancestor Gian Maria Galeazzo Sforza to the Duke of Ferrara conceding him twelve sacks of *risone*, as it was then called, with which to experiment in the wetlands of that province. For the first time, rice cultivation officially and legally began outside Lombardy. Although it has to be said that all the regulations and impositions which had been drawn up to prevent the distribution and cultivation of rice outside Lombardy had been largely ineffectual. By the time Ferrara received his permission from Sforza to plant the crop legally, cultivation was already under way in many other areas of the north.

Export took a great leap forward after this, as rice made its way north into the rest of Europe through the Gotthard Pass. In 1494, regulations were drawn up regarding the use of the Pass and the quantity of rice being sent abroad with the result that within five years there emerged a completely new breed of merchant specializing exclusively in the complicated export of rice grain. Traffic over the

Pass became so intense that Ludovico il Moro, who had by then supplanted Francesco Sforza as Duke of Milan, eventually banned the export of rice altogether. A notable statistic as an indication of this crop's importance at that time is that by 1550 rice fields occupied 550 hectares of land around the city of Milan.

This was largely due to a decision taken by Ludovico il Moro, Duke of Milan, in 1489, shortly after his accession to power. Before this, rice had been grown according to the Arabic technique, which favoured the dry-cultivation method.

Ludovico il Moro, Duke of Milan,
who introduced the growing
of rice plants in water into Italy
in the fifteenth century.

My ancestor Ludovico, ignoring all protestations and general consternation about public hygiene, ordered the most radically significant alteration to the method of cultivation of rice: the flooding of the fields so that the rice plants would grow in the water.

The main causes for public concern were all regarding personal health, and eventually led to a general mistrust of rice, as opposed to rice flour, altogether. Great efforts were made to try and remove the taint of 'illness' from this valuable crop. Even the Church became involved, including a declaration by Cardinal Carlo Borromeo dated 1576 in which he stated that there was no link between malaria and the rice fields. Eight years later, amidst continuing hysteria, the doctors of the College of Novara bravely published their conclusions regarding health and rice cultivation. Their findings, which were later proved to be absolutely correct, were that rice cultivation would not be hazardous to health provided the water in the fields was kept clear and running and was not permitted to turn stagnant and marshy.

Despite these assertions, however, the controversy raged on. On 24 September 1575, the Viceroy of Spain, Marquis of Ayamonte, declared it illegal to grow rice within six miles of the city walls of Milan and within five miles of other city walls. The penalties imposed were extremely severe and included three years in chains, rowing aboard a warship, or exile outside the area for the same number of years. It is interesting to note that for the aristocracy and the clergy, who actually owned the fields, the punishments were considerably less severe than for others. The clergy, who considered themselves outside the law in any case, continued vociferously to deny the link between rice and pestilence and demanded their right to plant whatever was most convenient.

However, though the rice fields were the property of the upper classes, rice as a food does not appear to have been considered fit for their high tables, and remained very much a food for the workers and peasants. From its early status as an exotic imported novelty which could only be afforded by the gentry, it had come to serve quite a different purpose.

Because of the need to keep the poor fed, the importance of rice was eventually re-established as, particularly towards the end of the Middle Ages and for some time thereafter, rice was generally regarded as a very useful way of filling the bellies of a population which was increasing all too rapidly, and thus placing too great a strain on the country's wheat supplies. Consequently, by sheer necessity, rice production again became more important, while other previously unknown grains, such as rye and buckwheat, were also introduced into the daily diet.

During the fifteenth and sixteenth centuries, a very significant difference occurred on the tables of the common people as they began radically to change their diet. Meat and other high-protein foods were gradually replaced with large quantities of carbohydrates and thus rice, polenta and thick soups lined with coarse bread became the symbols of the food of the poor, the peasants and working-class citizens. This style of cuisine is still referred to as *la cucina povera* and these days has achieved an elitist status on the tables of the smartest restaurants world-wide. Strange, and rather sad, to think that we have had to go nearly to the end of the twentieth century to discover that this way of eating was the most health-giving and satisfying all along.

As a testimonial to how hard hunger was beating at the door in those times, a document written in 1590 by the diarist Pompeo Viziani of Bologna records that groups of peasants were thrown out of the city where they had come begging for food from an already overstretched situation, but once locked outside the city walls were each issued with four ounces of rice per day to keep them quiet until the harvest.

Thus rice, just like other great Italian food inventions such as pasta, polenta and pizza, was considered unsuitable for the nobility, but rather a solution to the problems of famine. Because of this, very few rice recipes actually emerged from Italy around that time. We do know, however, that in the north the cooking methods were influenced by France and Spain. Rice would be boiled in stock until tender, then other ingredients, such as vegetables or a little meat or fish when they were available, were added to complete the dish. With typical Italian flair and innovation, it was therefore possible to make whatever protein was available go much further and help to create tasty, rib-sticking dishes with which to feed many mouths.

However, after this period of relatively wide cultivation and success, rice in Italy seemed to take a backward step in the popularity stakes. It again became the spurious focus of various health problems, such as malaria, plague and other diseases. By the seventeenth century, many public authorities prohibited the widening and development of the cultivated fields, and in some cases insisted that whole plantations be abandoned altogether for reasons of bad sanitation and 'pestilential air'. At that time, a whole series of diseases attributed to the 'corruption of the air' were sweeping through Italy and the medical profession of those days did not have the knowledge to understand or to deal with them. All manner of amazing causes were attributed to various diseases and as many extraordinary cures. Rice and its cultivation, which was just beginning to become established, seemed to be swept up in the general confusion and the mêlée of contradiction.

In the eighteenth century, however, the problems of feeding the hungry populace again became paramount and rice regained an important position in the Italian diet. Once again, the starchy foods became crucial and all over the country, rice and other crops such as maize, potatoes and buckwheat were either introduced or reintroduced. This was to be the turning point for rice, as it began to be eaten by a great many more people of all classes, and recipes began to appear more frequently in cookery books.

The old method of cooking rice in a pot of broth and adding a selection of other ingredients depending on when they were available was born largely out of necessity, but nonetheless had stood the test of time and been around for several hundred years. In the nineteenth century, however, the recipes which started to appear began to use the cooking method we know today: toasting the rice grains,

A painting by Angelo Morbelli of rice-planting in Italy during the late nineteenth century.

then gradually incorporating the hot stock. Who actually created the very first risotto as we know it? When did the switch happen from a simple boiling technique to a method which allows the rice to hold its shape, flavour and texture, while letting the accompanying ingredients not only mingle and blend, but also retain their own identity? I would love to be able to put down a name on this page of the unsung hero of a cook who achieved this vital step, but every one of the documents and books I have read omits this vital piece of information!

What we can record, however, is that by the nineteenth century, rice was completely embraced by the upper classes and it had taken its rightful place, principally in the form of risotto, as a major star in Italy's culinary firmament.

Types of Rice

In ancient Sanskrit, it was called *vrihi*. It then made its way into the Persian language where it appeared as *brizi*. From there it wended its way into the Greek kitchen and language as *oriza*. In the course of history, the food and the word became part of the Roman civilization with the name of *oryza*. Other early names include the southern Indian name of *arisi*, the Illirian *oryz* and the Arab *eruz* or *uruz*. We know it as rice.

An annual plant, rice stands alongside wheat as one of the staple foods for human nourishment. It belongs to the family of grains – with oats, wheat, barley and rye – but is actually rather different from all these, most importantly for us because of the composition of the starch it contains. It is this starch which creates the creamy velvet that makes a risotto.

Over thousands of years, the original rice grain eventually developed into two different cultivated species: the Asiatic *Oryza sativa* and the African *Oryza glaberrima*. The African variety was cultivated extensively along the upper Niger river and in the lands around Lake Chad as early as 1500 BC.

Oryza sativa, the more important of the two, gradually divided into three separate sub-species: Indica, Japonica and Javanica. As the name suggests, Indica is cultivated in India. It is a high-yielding and disease-resistant crop with a long, clean, clear, narrow grain. From this rice is derived the Pakistani variety called Basmati, with its characteristic sandalwood perfume; Thai rice; and all the long-grain American rices that come under the general heading of Patna. Japonica is the grain suitable for growth in more temperate climates. It has a short grain with plenty of starch and is often glutinous. Passing from China to Japan, it became, through hybridization, the source from which all the Italian rice varieties developed. Javanica, the least important type, is used mainly in Indonesia and has a long, very fat grain.

Until 1887, none of the rice grown and eaten in Italy had been given any particular name or classification, as all the varieties had developed as a result of spontaneous cross-fertilization.

However, in 1887, the first named rice variety was grown in the Vercelli area from a seed variety called Giapponino, but this was still very different from modern risotto rice. After this, three very specific rice varieties were developed – Nostrale, Originario and Lady Wright – which changed the face of Italian rice for ever. Nostrale was very well known throughout the nineteenth century; Chinese Originario was developed in 1904 from a Japanese seed called Omahi; and a grain called Lady Wright was imported from the USA in 1925. Further work and experimentation was carried out in cross-fertilization and hybridization until finally a wide range of Italian rices as we know them today was developed.

Even in very early Italian recipe books for risotto, dated in the first half of the twentieth century, the writers specified the particular rice variety required for each specific recipe. In other words, they considered, quite rightly, that certain rice types worked better with some ingredients than others. This remains true, of course, although these days, it is more difficult to find such a wide range of rice types suitable for risotto, so that many of our risotti are now quite different from those our grandmothers and great-grandmothers enjoyed.

These are the main risotto rice varieties which are currently available, but the development of further varieties continues, and the picture is still changing.

Arborio is an immensely popular variety and is the one which is the most readily available. It takes its name from the little town in the Vercelli area where it was first developed in 1946. Because it has a very large grain, it needs to be cooked with special care and in particular needs to be rested, off the heat, once almost cooked. This process is called *mantecare*. Arborio rice is suitable for all risotti, but can also be boiled, rinsed and dressed with butter and freshly grated Parmesan cheese or with a separately made sauce.

Baldo is a very fine rice with a compact structure. It is suitable for risotti, rice salads and boiled rice dressed with a separately prepared sauce.

Carnaroli is excellent for all risotti. The starch contained in this rice variety is the richest of all in the substance which allows the grain to keep its shape and texture. This makes it a relatively easy rice to cook and is the least likely to overcook and turn mushy.

Originario is considered suitable for rice dishes made with sausage, to accompany meat stews, and for vegetable risotti, baked rice dishes with either fish or aubergines and Mozzarella, rice cooked in milk, stuffing, *arancini* and rissoles.

Padano and **Maratelli** are good for soups and all kinds of risotto.

Ribe is best used for dishes that require boiled rice, but it can also be used for risotto.

Roma and **Sant'Andrea** are large-grained rices that are suitable for all traditional risotti and are used specifically for *Rise e Bisi*.

Rosa Marchetti is an extremely rare rice with a very distinctive, small, fairly rounded grain. Used mainly in the Piedmont, I have only ever been able to buy it in the Langhirano.

Vialone Nano is a rice variety which is most popular in the Mantova and Verona areas. It has a large, rounded grain. This is the rice to use if you want an extra creamy, smooth risotto.

Vialone Nano Gigante is a giant version of Vialone Nano. It has the same properties but a noticeably larger grain.

NOTES ON THE RECIPES

Spoon measurements are level.

1 tablespoon is 15 ml; 1 teaspoon is 5 ml.

Eggs are medium.

Wash fresh produce before preparation.

A wine glass is about 150 ml (5 fl oz).

Follow one set of measurements only;
do not mix metric and imperial.

Adjust seasoning or strongly flavoured
ingredients to taste.

The approximate proportions for a risotto are 100 g
(4 oz) of rice per person, although you should use
less rice if you have lots of other ingredients,
particularly if they are bulky.

For each portion, use about 10 g ($^{1}/_{4}$ oz) of onion
and 20 g ($^{3}/_{4}$ oz) of butter.

Use 1.5 litres ($2^{1}/_{2}$ pints) of stock for each 500 g
(1 lb 2 oz) of rice.

The portions specified tend to be fairly generous.

The Stock *Il Brodo*

I cannot emphasize enough just how important a quality stock is to a risotto. If you have a good stock with plenty of flavour, it is virtually impossible to make a bad, tasteless risotto. Throughout the book I have suggested what kind of stock is better with one or another recipe, although you may of course disagree and choose to use another type of stock from the one in the ingredients list. But whatever you use, remember that each grain of rice is capable of absorbing up to five times its own volume in liquid, so that means that all the flavour of the stock is going to be in the grains. In some cases, such as when making a fish risotto, it is obvious that a fish or vegetable stock is going to be more appropriate than a game or beef stock. In other instances, the most appropriate choice is less obvious. Think about the combination of flavours in your risotto and take everything into account when choosing which stock to select. When in doubt, use vegetable or light chicken stock. It is far better to use a weaker stock than an overpowering one. Particularly strong stocks like brown beef or game need very big accompanying flavours to take on their strength.

In all the recipes I have given a quantity of stock, but this can only be approximate. You may not use the whole quantity of stock, or on the other hand you may need a little more. This depends on the level of heat under the pan, the shape and size of the pan, the variety of rice you are using, and the other ingredients within the recipe such as wine or the juices from the vegetables. If you run out of stock, you can use simmering water or another glass of wine to finish off the cooking, or heat up more stock if you have any.

There should never be any need to use stock cubes for a risotto. You can freeze your own lovingly made stock in ice cube trays, then freeze the cubes in labelled bags. Remember to date the labels so as not to have any nasty surprises by discovering spoiled stock.

1

2

Place all the stock ingredients in a pan. Pour over the water and add the salt.

Bring to the boil, then lower the heat, cover and simmer for about 2 hours. Skim the surface frequently to remove any scum. Remove from the heat and leave to cool.

3

4

Strain the stock through a fine sieve into a bowl or jug, pressing down on the pieces in the sieve to extract every last bit of flavour.

When the stock has cooled completely it will be easy to remove any fat from the surface as it will have solidified. You can keep it in the fridge for up to 3 days or in the freezer for about 6 months.

Chicken Stock
Brodo di Pollo

MAKES ABOUT 1.5 LITRES (2½ PINTS)

about 750 g (1¾ lb) cooked or raw chicken

1 onion, quartered, or 1 leek, halved lengthways

2 celery sticks, halved

2 carrots, halved

1.5 litres (2½ pints) cold water

2 pinches of salt

a few sprigs of fresh parsley

6 black peppercorns

Method

Place the chicken and the vegetables in a stock pot, pour over the water and add the salt, parsley and peppercorns. Bring to the boil, then lower the heat, cover and simmer for about 2 hours. Skim the surface frequently to remove any scum. Remove from the heat and leave to cool.

Strain into a bowl or jug, pressing down on the pieces in the sieve to extract every last bit of flavour. When the stock has cooled completely it will be easy to remove any fat from the surface as it will have solidified. Keep in the fridge for up to 3 days or in the freezer for about 6 months.

Fish Stock
Brodo di Pesce

Only use white fish to make a delicately flavoured fish stock.

MAKES ABOUT 3 LITRES (5$^{1}/_{4}$ PINTS)

about 2 kg (4$^{1}/_{2}$ lb) assorted white fish
   trimmings and bones

1 leek, sliced

1 large celery stick, quartered

1 carrot, quartered

1 glass dry white wine

6 sprigs of fresh parsley

$^{1}/_{4}$ lemon

12 black peppercorns

2 bay leaves

2 pinches of salt

2.5 litres (4$^{1}/_{2}$ pints) cold water

Method

Soak all the raw fish in cold water for 10 minutes to remove any bitter or muddy taste, then rinse carefully. Remove and discard all gills and eyes.

Put all the fish in a stock pot. Add all the other ingredients, stir together and bring to the boil. Lower the heat, cover and simmer gently for no longer than 20 minutes, otherwise the stock might turn bitter. Skim off any scum which might appear on the surface during cooking. Remove from the heat and cool completely.

When it is cold, strain the stock into a bowl, pressing down on the ingredients to squeeze out all the flavour. It will keep in the fridge for about 2 days or in the freezer for about 3 months.

Beef or Veal Stock
Brodo di Manzo o di Vitello

MAKES ABOUT 3 LITRES (5¹/₄ PINTS)

1.5 kg (3 lb) beef or veal bones

1 onion, quartered

2 carrots, quartered

1 leek, quartered

2 celery sticks, quartered

1 tomato, quartered

1 bouquet garni, made up of sprigs
   of fresh parsley and thyme

6 black peppercorns

a pinch of salt

3 litres (5¹/₄ pints) cold water

Method

Place all the ingredients in a large stock pot. Bring to the boil, lower the heat, cover and simmer for about 4 hours, skimming off the scum which forms on the surface as it cooks.

Strain the stock, pressing down on the vegetables in the sieve to extract every little bit of flavour. Leave to cool. It will keep in the fridge for about 3 days or in the freezer for about 6 months.

For a richer, brown stock, roast the bones first in a roasting tin in a preheated oven at 230°C/450°F/gas mark 8 for about 20 minutes, then add the vegetables and cook for a further 20–25 minutes. Baste with a little water during cooking if necessary, then transfer to a stock pot, add the rest of the water and continue as described above.

Game or Duck Stock
Brodo di Cacciagione o di Anatra

 If you are making duck stock, use half the amount of butter.

MAKES ABOUT 2 LITRES (3¹/₂ PINTS)

40 g (1¹/₂ oz) butter

1 kg (2¹/₄ lb) carcasses of game or duck,
  coarsely chopped

500 g (1 lb 2 oz) mixed carrot, onion, celery,
  leek and fresh parsley, coarsely chopped

2 litres (3¹/₂ pints) cold water

a pinch of salt

2 black peppercorns

Method

Melt the butter in a stock pot and fry the carcass pieces over a low heat until browned to heighten their flavour. When they are well browned, add all the vegetables and fry together until all the vegetables are shiny. Add the water, salt and peppercorns and bring to the boil. Lower the heat, cover and simmer for about 2 hours, skimming frequently.

Strain the stock, pressing down on the ingredients in the sieve to extract every little bit of flavour. Leave to cool. It will keep in the fridge for about 3 days or in the freezer for about 6 months.

Vegetable Stock
Brodo Vegetale

You can use any vegetables you like for a stock. It is a good way to use up raw vegetables which are a bit tired or left over.

MAKES ABOUT 1 LITRE (1³/₄ PINTS)

2 carrots, quartered

1 large onion, halved

2 celery sticks, quartered

2 tomatoes, halved

2–3 cabbage leaves, quartered

¹/₂ leek, left whole

8 lettuce leaves, halved

2 pinches of salt

1.2 litres (2 pints) cold water

Method

Clean all the vegetables, then place them in a stock pot. Add the salt and pour over the water. Bring to the boil slowly, then lower the heat, cover and simmer for about 1¹/₂ hours.

Remove from the heat and cool completely. Strain into a bowl or large jug. Keep in the fridge for up to 3 days or in the freezer for about 6 months.

Making Risotto

Making risotto is rather like making love. You must be in tune with and in the mood for what is going on. Be receptive to all the little creaking, popping, crackling noises the rice will make when you toast it until almost singed. Then breathe out with it when you finally add the first liquid and the rice rewards you with a hissing column of steam – this is known as *il sospiro*, the sigh. Now, as you stir the rice around, you are gently caressing it into a creamy, smooth masterpiece, waiting for just the right moment each time before you provide it with more liquid to swell the grains until they are plump and juicy, swimming in a sea of velvet. And finally, when it is all over, you let it rest quietly for a few moments before serving triumphantly.

There is no fixed rule about texture. In the north-west of Italy (Lombardia and Piemonte) they tend to make their risotti quite dry compared to the softer, wetter texture of the Veneto. It seems the further east you travel, the looser and softer the risotti become. You must only make sure the texture of your risotto is the way you like it!

Types of Rice

I have given suggestions of rice varieties where appropriate throughout the book, and these are based on my own personal preferences. This is a guide-line, however, not a rule, as I appreciate it is hard to find the different rice varieties and they seem to come and go in the shops. Experiment with different types of rice if you can, so that you can see how they vary the texture of the finished dish.

If I have not advised a specific rice variety, such as Carnaroli, the recipe will just read 'risotto rice', which means you must choose from any variety suitable for risotto. If you cannot find the type specified, use another variety. The most commonly available risotto rice is Arborio, which you will find in any supermarket. Other varieties are Vialone Nano, Vialone Nano Gigante, Roma, Baldo, Rosa Marchetti and Carnaroli, to name the most common (see pages 18–21).

What Can Go Wrong?

The main thing that seems to go wrong is overcooking. Don't be afraid to take the risotto off the heat, even when the grains still feel quite hard. The rice will continue to cook, and therefore soften, as long as it is still hot. There are several other things to watch out for. The flavour of the stock will affect everything, so always use a good-quality stock. It is easy to overseason or underseason, so taste and adjust the seasoning before you leave to risotto to rest. Sometimes the risotto can be just too dry or too wet and soupy, so keep adding the stock very gradually just until the risotto is creamy and velvety but the rice grains are still firm to the bite. If you have used all the stock recommended in the recipe and the risotto is not ready, continue to add a little more hot stock, water or wine.

Making Risotto for a Party

If you are serving a risotto for guests, I am afraid that there is no way you can half-cook it in advance and then finish it off just before you want to serve it. This is bad practice and does nothing to enhance the reputation of this amazingly delicious dish. On a good Italian restaurant menu, you will see *20 minuti* in brackets next to the risotti. This means that somebody will make your risotto expressly for you in the proper time. In the case of a dinner party, you can fry the onion or garlic in advance and have all your other ingredients prepared. Then you can either excuse yourself for the 20 minutes or so that you need to heat up the ingredients and cook the rice, or ask some of your guests to come into the kitchen with you.

Using Leftovers

If you have risotto left over, you can make the most delicious *Risotto in Padella*. This means that the risotto is tipped into some sizzling hot oil or butter in a frying pan and pressed down to make a thick pancake. Let the rice cook on the base until golden and crisp, then flip it over and repeat on the other side.

Some cooks like to mix the cold, leftover risotto with a couple of beaten eggs to make a kind of *Risotto Frittata*. The egg binds the mixture together and so does make it easier to turn it over with splitting.

Alternatively, you could divide the leftover risotto into small walnut-sized balls and push a little Mozzarella into the centre of each one. Seal the holes with more risotto and roll the balls in beaten egg and breadcrumbs. Deep-fry the rice balls in piping hot oil until golden brown, then drain on kitchen paper. Serve hot or just warm as a canapé or snack. If you have some leftover cooked vegetables such as peas, mushrooms or similar, or some cured meat like prosciutto crudo, mortadella or salami, you could mix them into the rice too.

Short-cut Risotto

If 20 minutes just seems too long to wait, there are now a selection of 'quick-cook' Italian risotto products on the market which you might feel tempted to try. Made by one of Italy's oldest and certainly Italy's largest rice company, Riso Gallo, these ten-minute risotto ideas come in various different types, amongst which are saffron, cuttlefish ink, tomato, spinach and asparagus.

You should not think of any of these risotti as classic, properly made risotti, but they are exceptionally delicious and are certainly easier and quicker to pre-pare. Technically, they are real, traditionally made risotti with the moisture taken out. To cook, you simply add water, simmer and stir. Like I said, don't imagine it will ever be the same as a risotto you have made yourself from scratch as you'll never get the creamy texture of home-made risotto, but with a little imagination you can turn any of these products into a very agreeable, easy-to-prepare meal. For example, try adding cooked peas to the tomato risotto; cooked prawns to the cuttlefish ink; cooked mushrooms to the saffron; chopped Parma ham to the asparagus; or crumbled Gorgonzola cheese to the spinach.

Equipment for Making Risotto

You will need a stock pot for your stock or hot water. You will also need a really comfortable wooden spoon with which to do your gentle, rhythmic stirring. But most importantly you will need the right kind of pot in which to cook the risotto. It needs to be deep and wide, but not so deep that you can't stir comfortably, nor so wide that all the liquid evaporates really quickly before the rice has had a chance to absorb it. The best pans are wider than they are tall. Make sure the pan is large enough to cook all the risotto easily without the risk of slopping over the side whilst you stir, and that it has a good solid, even base so that the bottom of the risotto does not become too hot. It is not a good idea, on the whole, to use a non-stick pan because the risotto is meant to stick on the bottom while it cooks, but if you prefer to use non-stick, it won't make that much difference. Remember that many risotti need to rest under a lid, so make sure your chosen pot has a lid which fits well.

STEP BY STEP TO THE PERFECT RISOTTO

These guidelines are for the majority of risotti contained in this book, although a few recipes use a different cooking method.

The first thing to do is to choose the correct size pan. Make sure it is large enough for all the rice once it is cooked, plus the other ingredients which are included in the recipe.

1

2

Fry the onion, and garlic or other vegetables if using, without allowing them to brown.

Add the rice and toast it carefully until shiny, opaque and very hot, but again without letting it brown. Stir continuously and be patient.

Begin to add the wine or the first ladleful of hot stock only when the rice is at its hottest. Stir it into the rice and keep stirring until it has all been absorbed. Continue to add the hot stock a ladleful at a time. Always wait for the liquid to be absorbed before adding more. Don't hurry this process; let the rice soak up the liquid and the corresponding flavour at its own pace. Regulate your heat accordingly, keeping the pan over a roughly medium heat. Stir constantly.

Prepare all your ingredients before you start to cook. Check your stock for flavour, colour and so on to make sure it is the right kind of stock for the risotto you plan to make. Choose the correct rice for the recipe. Heat the stock and keep it just at simmering point.

3

4

Gradually you will see that the spoon will leave a clear wake behind it as it is drawn through the risotto. This is a sign of the rice being cooked or almost cooked. It will probably stick to the centre of the pan slightly.

The risotto is cooked when the texture is velvety but each grain is still firm to the bite in the centre. At this point, most recipes tell you to take the risotto off the heat, stir in extra butter and/or cheese and cover the pot. Leaving the risotto to rest in this way is called *mantecare* and it makes the texture even more creamy and smooth. After resting, turn out on to a warmed platter or warmed individual dishes and serve at once.

1 Cheese and Egg

This chapter includes the simplest risotto of all, Cheese and Butter Risotto, (page 40), one which I feel is a good test of one's risotto-making skills. It is all too easy to hide a technical mistake or moment of laziness under a heap of impressive ingredients!

The Savoury Rice Cake on page 45 can also be made in individual timbale moulds or ramekins but it does look good as a large cake turned out of a cake tin. If you feel nervous about turning it out, simply leave it in the tin and cut out wedges.

The Fontina and Gorgonzola recipes (pages 39 and 42) both illustrate a way of using strong-tasting cheese on its own to make a risotto. Do feel free to experiment with other cheeses, which might not even be Italian, but bear in mind that the blandness of the rice itself and the taste of the stock you use will automatically mean you must use a cheese with plenty of flavour.

Fontina Risotto
Risotto alla Fontina

In Valle d'Aosta, I have eaten some versions of this recipe which involved a lot of egg yolks and cream as well as plenty of this marvellously rich cheese. I have since worked out a recipe which is rich without being overwhelming!

SERVES 4

1 onion, chopped

$^1/_2$ garlic clove, chopped

100 g (4 oz) unsalted butter

400 g (14 oz) risotto rice, preferably
  Vialone Nano

1 glass fruity, German-style white wine

1.2 litres (2 pints) chicken stock,
  kept simmering

120 g (4$^1/_2$ oz) Fontina cheese, cubed

sea salt and freshly milled black pepper

Method

Fry the onion and garlic in half the butter over a low heat until the onion has practically dissolved but has not browned. Stir in the rice and raise the heat a little so that as you turn the rice in the butter and onion it becomes coated, hot and toasted. Do not let any of the ingredients brown. Pour in the wine and simmer until the alcohol has evaporated and the grains have absorbed the flavour of the wine. Then begin to add the hot stock, stirring constantly and allowing the liquid to be absorbed before adding more. When you have added half the stock and the rice is about half cooked, stir in the cheese so that it is evenly distributed through the risotto. Continue to cook the rice, making sure that the rice always absorbs the stock before you add more liquid. This will take about 20 minutes in all. When the risotto is creamy and velvety but the rice grains are still firm to the bite, adjust the seasoning with salt and pepper, make sure all the cheese has melted through the risotto, then remove from the heat. Stir in the remaining butter, cover and leave to rest for about 2 minutes. Stir one more time, then transfer to a warmed platter and serve at once.

Cheese and Butter Risotto
Risotto alla Parmigiana

This plain and simple risotto makes a very good base for all kinds of other additions. Master this one and you can make any kind of risotto!

SERVES 6

1 onion, finely chopped

75 g (3 oz) unsalted butter

500 g (1 lb 2 oz) risotto rice,
    preferably Vialone Nano

1.5 litres (2½ pints) chicken, meat
    or flavoursome vegetable stock,
    kept simmering

50 g (2 oz) Parmesan cheese, freshly grated

sea salt and freshly milled black pepper

Method

Fry the onion in half the butter for about 10 minutes over a very low heat until is soft but not coloured. Stir in the rice and toast the grains thoroughly on all sides so that they are opaque but not coloured. Add the first ladleful of hot stock and stir it in. Then continue adding the stock a ladleful at a time, letting the rice absorb the liquid and all its flavour before adding more, and stirring continously. This will take about 20 minutes. When the risotto is almost completely soft and creamy but the rice grains are still firm to the bite, stir in the remaining butter and the cheese. Taste and adjust the seasoning, then cover and leave to rest for about 3 minutes before transferring to a warmed platter to serve.

Gorgonzola Risotto
Risotto al Gorgonzola

The very strong taste of good, ripe Gorgonzola is unmistakable and absolutely delicious. If you find it a little too strong, try using half the quantity or alternatively use Dolcelatte, which is younger than Gorgonzola by about six months but is still the same cheese. Incidentally, Dolcelatte is only made for foreign export. Follow this risotto with a mouth-cleansing rocket salad with orange.

SERVES 4

1 onion, chopped

1/2 teaspoon dried sage leaves, very finely chopped

100 g (4 oz) unsalted butter

400 g (14 oz) risotto rice

1.2 litres (2 pints) chicken or vegetable stock, kept simmering

100 g (4 oz) ripe Gorgonzola cheese, diced

2 tablespoons single cream

4 fresh sage leaves, very finely chopped

sea salt and freshly milled black pepper

a few fried sage leaves to garnish

freshly grated Parmesan cheese to serve

Method

Fry the onion and dried sage together in half the butter until the onion is soft and melting but not browned. Add all the rice and raise the heat slightly to toast the grains, stirring so that they are covered with onion, sage and butter. Don't let any of the ingredients brown but make sure you get the rice really hot before adding the first ladleful of stock. Begin to add the hot stock, stirring constantly and allowing the liquid to be absorbed before adding more. When you have added half the stock, stir in the cheese. It will melt quickly and soon become distributed through the rice if you keep stirring. Continue to cook the rice, making sure that the grains always absorb the stock before you add more liquid. This will take about 20 minutes in all. When the risotto is creamy and velvety but the rice grains are still firm to the bite, remove from the heat and stir in the remaining butter, the cream and the fresh sage. Adjust the seasoning, bearing in mind that Gorgonzola is very salty so you probably won't need to add more salt, though you will probably like a little pepper. Cover and leave to rest for 2 minutes, then turn out on to a warm platter, garnish with the fried sage leaves and serve at once with the Parmesan offered separately.

Egg Risotto
Risotto all'Uovo

There is more than one version of this very simple, nourishing and delicious *risotto casalingo*, or home-cooked risotto. It reminds me so much of cold evenings when the Tuscan damp seemed to pervade every seam of the house and all I wanted to do was snuggle up to the fire with a warm bowl of food. You may need to add some more stock or to drain off some stock at the end of the rice cooking time; it depends of the quality of the rice you choose.

SERVES 6

1.5 litres (2^1/$_2$ pints) chicken stock

500 g (1 lb 2 oz) risotto rice

6 fresh free-range eggs

120 g (4^1/$_2$ oz) Parmesan cheese, freshly grated

sea salt and freshly milled black pepper

2 tablespoons unsalted butter

Method

Bring the stock to the boil and throw in the rice. Stir and simmer gently for about 20 minutes until just tender. It really must be *al dente*. Beat the eggs with the Parmesan and season with salt and pepper. Butter a serving bowl very thoroughly with half the butter. When the rice is ready, pour in the egg mixture and stir thoroughly. Pour the rice into the bowl and stir, then add the remaining butter and stir again. Transfer to a warmed platter and serve immediately.

Savoury Rice Cake
Torta di Riso Salata

For this cake you'll need one of those new, flavoured risotto rices. In fact, what they are is a risotto that has been made and then dehydrated to form a flavoured, partly-cooked rice. It sounds a bit strange, and I am the first to say that we are not talking about real risotto in this case, but these products do offer a much quicker solution than slow stirring and are useful for recipes like this one. I also have to say that they are delicious to eat and can be a lot nicer than some so-called 'real' risotti offered in restaurants. The cake is usually served as a main course, or as one of several dishes in a grand buffet.

MAKES ONE 25 CM/10 IN CAKE

butter for greasing

2 tablespoons semolina

150 g (5 oz) risotto rice flavoured
  with tomato or spinach

1.25 litres (2¼ pints) chicken stock,
  kept simmering

6 eggs, beaten

6 ripe, sweet tomatoes, skinned,
  seeded and diced

150 g (5 oz) fresh Mozzarella cheese, cubed

75 g (3 oz) Parmesan cheese, freshly grated

sea salt and freshly milled black pepper

2 tomatoes, thinly sliced

Method

Preheat the oven to 180°C/350°C/gas mark 4. Butter a deep 25 cm (10 in) cake tin and sprinkle generously with semolina.

Put the risotto rice in a pan and cook with about two-thirds of the stock for about 5 minutes until just beginning to go tender. Remove from the heat and stir in the remaining stock, then leave to cool slightly. Add the eggs, diced tomatoes, Mozzarella and Parmesan. Season to taste with salt and pepper, then turn into the prepared tin. Arrange the sliced tomatoes on the top and bake in the centre of the oven for about 30 minutes until a knife inserted into the centre of the cake comes out clean. Turn out of the tin and serve warm. (If you are nervous about turning the cake out, serve straight from the tin.)

2 *Vegetables*

Summer is the best time to make many of the huge range of vegetable risotti, as vegetables are plentiful, varied and many are often at their best during this season. However, this is not to say that I have excluded from my repertoire all the autumn and winter vegetables such as pumpkin, cabbage, cardoon, potato, chard and spinach. I have included all the risotto recipes which include vegetables that I think work best in this context. In other words, the ones I like best!

One of the things I like best about shopping at markets, especially in Italy, is that the fantastic array of vegetables and fruits spilling off the stalls gives you all the inspiration you could ever need to create the most wonderful dishes. I never go to a market with the intention of buying specific items. I am there to be seduced and bewitched into making decisions by the colours, smells, textures and flavours of the produce on display.

Try using that philosophy with a risotto: buy the vegetables which attract and inspire you the most, then build the risotto around them. If your chosen vegetables don't appear in this collection, then I'm sure you could adapt. For example, I have not included a parsnip risotto, but I know it tastes good, so just use the potato recipe (page 63) and substitute parsnips for the potatoes. The same recipe will also work (although it is likely to be a little sweet) with yams, if you happen to like them, or even Jerusalem artichokes.

Risotto with Artichokes
Risotto ai Carciofi

SERVES 4

8 large, fresh globe artichokes

I lemon, quartered

I small onion, finely chopped

75 g (3 oz) prosciutto crudo,
   finely chopped

a handful of fresh flatleaf parsley,
   finely chopped

75 g (3 oz) unsalted butter

I glass dry white wine

sea salt and freshly milled black pepper

400 g (14 oz) Arborio rice

1.2 litres (2 pints) chicken or vegetable
   stock, kept simmering

50 g (2 oz) Parmesan cheese,
   freshly grated

Method

Remove and discard all the external leaves from the artichokes. Cut the artichokes in half and then into quarters. Rub the cut artichokes thoroughly with the cut lemons to prevent them from turning brown. Remove the hairy chokes from the centre and cut the artichokes into thin strips. Put the sliced artichokes into a basin of cold water with the lemon quarters until required.

Fry the onion gently with the prosciutto, parsley and half the butter until the onion is soft but not browned. Drain the artichokes carefully, then rub them in a cloth to dry them. Add them to the onion, stir together and simmer gently for about 10 minutes until the artichokes are tender, basting occasionally with the wine. Season with salt and pepper. Add the rice and stir together until the rice is crackling hot. Pour in the first ladleful of hot stock. Stir together and allow the rice to absorb the liquid, then add the next ladleful of stock. Continue in this way, stirring and adding stock a ladleful at a time. This will take about 20 minutes. When the risotto is creamy but the rice grains are still firm in the centre, remove from the heat and stir in the remaining butter and the Parmesan. Adjust the seasoning to taste, then cover and leave to rest for about 3 minutes. Transfer to a warmed platter and serve at once.

Asparagus Risotto
Risotto d'Asparagi

SERVES 6

500 g (1 lb 2 oz) fresh asparagus

sea salt

2 large shallots, chopped

75 g (3 oz) unsalted butter

500 g (1 lb 2 oz) risotto rice

1.5 litres (2½ pints) chicken or vegetable stock, kept simmering

50 g (2 oz) Parmesan cheese, freshly grated

1 tablespoon chopped fresh parsley

freshly milled black pepper

Method

Bring a pan of water to the boil with a large pinch of salt. Add the asparagus and boil for about 6 minutes or until just tender. Drain, reserving the cooking liquid, and leave the asparagus to cool. Cut the asparagus into small pieces, leaving the heads intact. If the ends of any of the asparagus stalks are very tough, scrape out the inside with a knife and discard the rest. Reheat the cooking liquid.

Fry the shallots in half the butter for about 5 minutes until soft and transparent. Add the rice all in one go and stir it around until it is heated through and shining. Then add the first ladleful of hot asparagus cooking liquid. Stir until the liquid has been absorbed, then add some more. Always add small amounts and always wait for the rice to absorb the liquid before you add any more. When you run out of the cooking liquid, begin to add the hot stock a ladleful at a time. Continue in this way for about 20 minutes, stirring in the asparagus to heat through right at the end of cooking. When the risotto is creamy and velvety and the rice grains are swollen but still firm to the bite, stir in the Parmesan and parsley and season to taste with pepper. Remove from the heat, cover and leave to stand for about 3 minutes. Transfer to a warmed serving platter and serve at once.

Aubergine Risotto
Risotto di Melanzane

Before you decide to make this risotto, bear in mind that the aubergine needs about 45 minutes' draining time. I like to finish off the dish with a few slices of aubergine, coated in flour and fried, laid on the top just before serving.

SERVES 4–6

400 g (14 oz) aubergines

sea salt

1 onion, chopped

3 garlic cloves, finely chopped

a handful of fresh flatleaf parsley, finely chopped

5 tablespoons extra virgin olive oil

freshly milled black pepper

1.5 litres (2½ pints) chicken or vegetable stock, kept simmering

500 g (1 lb 2 oz) risotto rice

a pinch of dried oregano

2 tablespoons freshly grated Pecorino cheese

2 tablespoons fresh Ricotta cheese

Method

Cut the aubergines into cubes and lay them all in a colander. Cover them with salt and put a plate on top. Place a weight on the plate and put the colander in the sink for about 45 minutes to allow the bitter juices from the aubergines to be released and drain away. Wash the aubergines thoroughly and dry them in a clean cloth.

Fry the onion, garlic and parsley in the oil until the onion is soft but not browned. Add the aubergine cubes and fry gently for a few minutes. Season with pepper and cook for about 10 minutes until the aubergines are soft, basting occasionally with a little stock to keep the mixture moist. Add the rice and stir until the rice is heated through but not browned. Add the hot stock a ladleful at a time, stirring until the stock is absorbed into the rice. Continue in this way, stirring and gradually adding the stock. This will take about 20 minutes. When the rice is tender but still firm in the centre of the grains and the risotto is creamy, remove from the heat and stir in the oregano, the Pecorino and Ricotta. Stir together thoroughly, cover and leave to rest for 1 minute. Turn out on to a warmed platter and serve at once.

Bean and Cabbage Risotto
Risotto Valtellinese

A very substantial risotto, this reflects the eating habits of mountain inhabitants who are used to sub-zero temperatures. Not only delicious, it is also immensely comforting. Fresh borlotti beans, if you can find them, need to be treated in the same way as dried ones.

SERVES 4

300 g (11 oz) fresh or dried borlotti beans, soaked overnight in cold water

300 g (11 oz) Savoy or green cabbage leaves

400 g (14 oz) risotto rice

sea salt and freshly milled black pepper

75 g (3 oz) Parmesan cheese, freshly grated

5 fresh sage leaves, finely chopped

2 tablespoons unsalted butter

Method

Rinse the soaked beans in clean water, then tip them into a pan and cover generously with cold water. Bring to the boil and boil vigorously for 5 minutes, then drain and rinse. Boil again in fresh water until soft, 20–30 minutes for fresh or 45–60 minutes for dried. Drain and discard the water.

Bring another pan of salted water (about 1.5 litres (2½ pints)) to the boil, then plunge the cabbage leaves into the boiling water for 1 minute. Scoop them out, drain well and chop finely. Add the rice to the boiling water, then stir in the chopped cabbage. Season with salt and pepper and boil gently for about 20 minutes until the rice is cooked but still firm to the bite and the water has been absorbed. Stir in the beans and heat through, then remove from the heat. Stir in the Parmesan, sage and butter and adjust the seasoning to taste. Cover and leave to rest for 2 minutes, then stir once more and transfer to a warmed bowl to serve.

Beetroot Risotto
Risotto di Rape Rosse

The amazing thing about this risotto is, of course, the stunning heliotrope colour. Please make sure you use beetroot which has been cooked in water and not in vinegar. Don't overcook the beetroot or it will begin to go pale and uneven in colour.

SERVES 4–6

1 large onion, finely chopped

75 g (3 oz) unsalted butter

500 g (1 lb 2 oz) boiled beetroot, peeled and diced

500 g (1 lb 2 oz) Arborio rice

½ glass dry vermouth

1.5 litres (2½ pints) chicken or light duck stock, kept simmering

sea salt and freshly milled black pepper

3 tablespoons finely snipped fresh chives

3 tablespoons finely chopped fresh flatleaf parsley

75 g (3 oz) Parmesan cheese, freshly grated

Method

Fry the onion gently in half the butter until soft but not browned. Stir in the beetroot and cook for a few minutes until the beetroot is beginning to go quite soft and floppy. Add the rice and stir thoroughly until it is heated through and shining. Pour over the vermouth and boil for 1 minute to allow the alcohol to evaporate. Begin to add the stock a ladleful at a time in the usual way, stirring and waiting for the rice to absorb the liquid before adding more. When you have added half the stock, season to taste with salt and pepper, then continue adding the stock. This will take about 20 minutes in all. When the rice feels soft and fluffy and the risotto is creamy but the rice grains are still firm to the bite, remove from the heat. Stir in the remaining butter, most of the herbs and the Parmesan. Cover and leave to rest for 2–3 minutes, then transfer to a warmed platter, sprinkle with the remaining herbs and serve immediately.

Cardoon Risotto
Risotto ai Cardi

I think cardoons have to be one of my three favourite vegetables, and I miss them desperately because in Italy I was able to get them so easily all winter long. For this recipe, the cardoons need to be as white as possible, which means exposed to a hard frost, and you don't need much. This is a real world-class risotto! There is nothing which quite matches their flavour, but if you really can't find them, the nearest equivalent would be to use poached celeriac.

SERVES 4–6

2 cardoon sticks, white and tender

juice of 1 lemon

2 tablespoons plain flour

4 tablespoons single cream

sea salt and freshly milled black pepper

75 g (3 oz) unsalted butter

1 onion, chopped

400 g (14 oz) risotto rice

1 glass dry sherry

1 glass dry white wine

1.2 litres (2 pints) chicken stock, kept simmering

4 tablespoons freshly grated Parmesan cheese,
  plus extra for serving

Method

Cut the cardoons into chunks and place them immediately in a pan of water with the lemon juice to stop them discolouring. Drain, cover with fresh water and sprinkle the flour into the water. Bring to the boil, then simmer gently for about 20 minutes until tender. Drain and rinse, then divide in half. Cut half the cardoons into cubes. Put the rest into a food processor with the cream and process until smooth. Season with salt and pepper and set aside. Melt one-third of the butter and fry the cardoon cubes quickly until golden, then set aside.

Now begin the risotto itself. Fry the onion in half the remaining butter until the onion is soft but not browned. Add the rice and stir until the grains are crackling hot. Add the sherry, stir and simmer for about 2 minutes for the rice to absorb the flavour, then add the wine and stir again. Begin to add the hot stock, stirring and waiting for the rice to absorb each ladleful of stock before adding more. This will take about 20 minutes. When the risotto is creamy and velvety but the grains are still firm to the bite, stir in the cardoon purée, then add the cardoon cubes and heat through. Adjust the seasoning to taste, then remove from the heat. Stir in the remaining butter and the Parmesan, cover and leave to rest for 2 minutes. Transfer to a warmed platter and serve at once with extra grated Parmesan offered separately.

Carrot and Orange Risotto
Risotto Arancione

What I like best about this dish is the lovely orange colour. Make sure you use good, juicy oranges and, if possible, organic carrots, which taste so much better than any others. Follow the risotto with a watercress salad to balance out the flavours.

SERVES 4

1 small onion, finely chopped

2 carrots, very finely chopped

100 g (4 oz) unsalted butter

400 g (14 oz) risotto rice

1 glass very dry white wine

1.2 litres (2 pints) chicken or
   vegetable stock, kept simmering

juice and finely grated zest of 2 oranges

juice of 1/2 lemon

1 boiled carrot, finely mashed

sea salt and freshly milled black pepper

3 tablespoons freshly grated Parmesan
   cheese

a few leaves of fresh mint, finely chopped

Method

Fry the onion and chopped carrots together gently in half the butter until very soft. Add the rice and stir around to coat the grains and make sure the rice is very hot without browning. Pour in the wine and stir until the grains have absorbed the liquid but the alcohol has evaporated. Now add the first ladleful of hot stock and stir it in, making sure the rice absorbs the liquid. Continue in this way, adding stock, stirring and waiting for absorption, until you have added half the stock. Stir in the orange juice and zest, the lemon juice and the mashed carrot. Adjust the seasoning with salt and pepper and continue to cook as before, adding stock and stirring. After about 20 minutes in all, the risotto will be velvety smooth but the grains will still feel firm to the bite. Remove from the heat and stir in the remaining butter and the Parmesan. Cover and leave to rest for 2 minutes, then transfer to a warmed platter and sprinkle with mint to serve.

Risotto with Courgettes and their Flowers
Risotto con Zucchine e Fiori

This risotto looks really stunning if you finish it off with a few deep-fried courgette flowers or deep-fried slices of courgette arranged on the top just before the risotto goes to the table (see page 60). The crisp, golden batter looks and tastes fantastic against the smooth, sweet, creaminess of the risotto.

SERVES 6

5 tablespoons olive oil

7 young, tender courgettes, very thinly sliced, with their flowers if possible

500 g (1 lb 2 oz) risotto rice

sea salt and freshly milled black pepper

1.5 litres (2$^1/_2$ pints) vegetable or chicken stock, kept simmering

25 g (1 oz) unsalted butter

50 g (2 oz) Parmesan cheese, freshly grated

Method

In a large, deep frying pan or wide pan, heat the oil and fry the sliced courgettes and flowers for about 5 minutes until tender. Add the rice and stir it around until coated with oil, heated through and shining. Season with salt and pepper, then begin to add the hot stock, stirring continously. Never add more than one ladleful of liquid at a time and wait for the rice to absorb it before adding any more. You may not need to add all the liquid, depending on the quality of the rice. This will take about 20 minutes from the time you start adding the liquid. When the risotto is creamy and velvety but the rice grains are still firm to the bite, remove from the heat. Season generously with salt and pepper, stir in the butter and Parmesan, cover and leave to rest for 2 minutes. Transfer to a warmed platter and serve immediately.

Fried Courgette Flowers
Fiori di Zucchini Fritti

Serve these on their own as an antipasto, or as a garnish on a pasta or risotto dish. If you want a really punchy flavour, add a small piece of canned anchovy fillet to the Mozzarella cubes, or for a really smooth, sweet flavour, fill the flowers with Ricotta. The same batter can be used to fry slices of courgette. It is useful to have quite a long stalk on the flowers.

FOR 12–14 FLOWERS

100 g (4 oz) Mozzarella cheese, cubed

12 courgette flowers, pistils removed,
  washed and carefully dried

1 egg, separated and the white chilled

40 g (1½ oz) plain flour

120 ml (4 fl oz) milk or milk and water

500 ml (17 fl oz) sunflower oil

sea salt

Method

Divide the Mozzarella between the courgette flowers, putting a few cubes into each cavity. Beat the egg yolk, flour and milk or milk and water together to make a smooth paste. Whisk the egg white until stiff, then fold into the batter.

Holding the flowers by their stalks, dip them into the batter to coat thoroughly. Use the batter as a sort of glue to fold and hold the petals of each flower so that the Mozzarella is secure inside.

Heat the oil in a wide, deep pan until a small piece of bread dropped into the oil sizzles instantly. Carefully place the courgette flowers in the oil and fry until crisp and golden all over, turning frequently. If the oil is hot enough this will only take about 4 minutes. Drain thoroughly on kitchen paper, sprinkle with a little salt and serve at once.

Fennel Risotto
Risotto di Finocchi

I have suggested adding aniseed liqueur to this recipe only to heighten the liquorice flavour of the fennel. If you want less of liquorice taste, leave out the aniseed liqueur. As an alternative, try a couple of tablespoons of Limoncello instead. In Italy, a great fuss is made over using male or female fennel bulbs, as the female (the whiter, fatter one with smooth, rounded buttocks) is considered far superior. Recognizing one from the other is an art I am still mastering under the careful tutelage of my endlessly patient family . . .

SERVES 4

500 g (1 lb 2 oz) fennel bulbs

1 onion, finely chopped

75 g (3 oz) unsalted butter

500 g (1 lb 2 oz) Arborio rice

2–3 tablespoons dry aniseed liqueur (optional)

sea salt and freshly milled black pepper

1.5 litres (2½ pints) chicken or vegetable stock, kept simmering

75 g (3 oz) Parmesan cheese, freshly grated

Method

Having established the sex of your fennel bulbs, take off all the hard external leaves and trim away all the green bits. You should be left with tender, white fennel hearts. Slice these thinly and evenly.

Fry the fennel and onion in half the butter for about 5 minutes until the fennel is tender. Add the rice and stir it around until it is heated through and shining. Add the liqueur, if using, and stir again. Season generously with salt and pepper, then begin gradually to add the hot stock a ladleful at a time, allowing the rice to absorb the liquid before adding more. Keep stirring and adding stock for about 20 minutes until the rice is creamy and cooked, though the grains must stay firm in the centre. When you reach this stage, stir in the remaining butter and the Parmesan. Cover and remove from the heat, then leave the rice to rest for about 2 minutes. Stir once more before transferring to a warmed platter to serve.

Roasted Pepper Risotto
Risotto ai Peperoni Arrosto

What is so delicious about this dish is the lovely sweet flavour of the roasted peppers. What makes it look so good is the brilliance of the colours. For these two reasons, I would recommend that you use either yellow or red peppers and avoid the green ones which can turn bitter and definitely lose all their colour once they are cooked.

SERVES 6

3 juicy red or yellow peppers

1 onion, finely chopped

1–2 garlic cloves, crushed

75 g (3 oz) unsalted butter

500 g (1 lb 2 oz) risotto rice

1.5 litres (2¹/₂ pints) vegetable or chicken stock, kept simmering

sea salt and freshly milled black pepper

75 g (3 oz) Parmesan cheese, freshly grated

Method

Preheat the grill to medium.

Grill the peppers all over, turning frequently until the outer skin is well blackened. Wrap them in clingfilm while they are still warm and leave to stand for about 10 minutes. Hold the peppers under running cold water and rub off the outer skin using a clean, new scouring pad. When the peppers are completely skinned their flesh will probably appear quite brown, which is as they should be. Cut them in half and remove all the inner seeds and membranes, then cut all the peppers into thin strips and put them aside for the moment.

Fry the onion and garlic very gently in the butter in a large, heavy-based pan until the onion is soft and transparent, then add the peppers and stir together gently over a low heat for about 5 minutes. Add the rice all in one go and stir together until the rice grains are coated and toasted all over. Then add the first ladleful of hot stock and stir it in; you should get a wonderful column of steam and an audible sigh of relief from the rice. Continue in this way for about 20 minutes, gradually adding stock and stirring it in until the rice grains are plump and tenderly swollen. Stir in seasoning to taste and add the Parmesan. Take off the heat, cover and leave to stand for about 3 minutes before transferring to a warmed platter to serve.

Potato Risotto
Risotto di Patate

If you really cannot find pancetta, you can substitute best-quality smoked streaky bacon, although nothing quite matches the taste of the real thing.

SERVES 4–6

120 g (4½ oz) pancetta, chopped

1 large onion, chopped

a handful of fresh flatleaf parsley, chopped

1 tablespoon fresh rosemary leaves, finely chopped

300 g (11 oz) potatoes, peeled and cubed

1.5 litres (2½ pints) beef or game stock, kept simmering

400 g (14 oz) Arborio rice

sea salt and freshly milled black pepper

50 g (2 oz) unsalted butter

50 g (2 oz) Groviera or Gruyère cheese, finely cubed

75 g (3 oz) Parmesan cheese, freshly grated

Method

Fry the pancetta gently with the onion, parsley and rosemary until the onion is soft and transparent but not browned. Add the potatoes and stir. Add 1–2 spoonfuls of stock to keep the contents of the pan moist and cook the potatoes for about 5 minutes until they lose their raw appearance. Add the rice and stir until the grains are shiny and opaque. Add the first ladleful of hot stock, stir and wait for the rice to absorb the liquid, then add more stock. Continue in this way for about 20 minutes until the rice is creamy and smooth, but make sure the grains remain firm in the centre. Take off the heat and season with salt and pepper. Stir in the butter and cheeses, cover and leave to rest for 3 minutes. Mix together once more, making sure the Groviera is melted and stringy, then turn on to a warmed platter and serve at once.

Pumpkin Risotto
Risotto alla Zucca

Pumpkin recipes are especially linked with the city of Mantova where they are used to make soups, sweet and savoury cakes, ravioli, gnocchi and this superb recipe for a delectably orange, creamy risotto. In Italy, greengrocers allow you to buy a piece off a pumpkin by weight so you only ever need to have as much as you need – a most sensible idea.

SERVES 4

75 g (3 oz) thickly cut pancetta or best-
   quality smoked streaky bacon, cubed

1 onion, chopped

500 g (1 lb 2 oz) pumpkin, peeled,
   seeded and chopped

400 g (14 oz) risotto rice

1.2 litres (2 pints) vegetable or chicken stock,
   kept simmering

sea salt and freshly milled black pepper

a handful of fresh flatleaf parsley, finely chopped

25 g (1 oz) unsalted butter

4 tablespoons freshly grated
   Parmesan cheese

Method

Fry the pancetta or bacon gently in a large heavy-based pan until the fat runs, then add the onion and fry until softened but not browned. Add the pumpkin and cook gently with the onion and pancetta for about 10 minutes until softened and mushy. Add the rice and toast it carefully on all sides, then begin to add the first ladleful of hot stock, stir and allow the rice to absorb the liquid. Add more stock, season to taste, and when the rice has absorbed the liquid, add more. Continue in this way for about 20 minutes until the rice is tender and all the grains are plump and cooked through. Stir in the parsley, butter and Parmesan, remove from the heat and cover. Leave to stand for 3 minutes, then transfer to a warmed platter and serve at once.

Radicchio Risotto
Risotto al Radicchio

Ideally, you must use the long, elegant *radicchio di Treviso* for this recipe, as it has a much better flavour than the other two versions which are squatter and smaller. A good alternative would be chicory, known in America as Belgian endive, and in Italy as *la Belga*. The taste of cooked radicchio is quite bitter, so you may like to use a slightly less than bone-dry wine to help redress the balance.

SERVES 4

1 onion, finely chopped

75 g (3 oz) unsalted butter

2 tablespoons fruity olive oil

400 g (14 oz) Arborio rice

1 glass red wine (not too dry)

400 g (14 oz) radicchio, washed
   and dried, then finely shredded

sea salt and freshly milled black pepper

1.5 litres (2¹/₂ pints) chicken or vegetable
   stock, kept simmering

1 teaspoon fresh rosemary leaves,
   finely chopped

2 tablespoons finely chopped fresh
   flatleaf parsley

50 g (2 oz) Parmesan cheese, freshly grated

Method

Fry the onion gently in half the butter and the oil until soft and transparent. Add the rice and mix together to cover the rice in oil, butter and onion. Stir until hot. Pour over the wine and stir thoroughly for 1 minute. Add the radicchio, mix together thoroughly and season with salt and pepper. Add the first ladleful of hot stock, stir and wait for the rice to absorb the liquid before adding more stock. Continue to cook the rice in this way, adding stock, stirring and adding more only when the previous stock as been absorbed into the rice. Add the rosemary and when the rice is creamy and tender but still firm at the centre of the grains, after about 20 minutes, remove from the heat. Stir in the remaining butter, the parsley and Parmesan. Cover and leave the risotto to rest for 2 minutes, then stir again and transfer to a warmed platter. Serve at once.

Savoy Cabbage Risotto
Risotto di Verze

This recipe has one of those lovely old-fashioned flavours, but with the very distinctive taste of caraway just to lift it. It originates from Friuli, where caraway is often added to flavour various dishes.

SERVES 6–8

1 onion, finely chopped

75 g (3 oz) unsalted butter
  or pork dripping

700 g (1 1/2 lb) risotto rice

2 glasses dry white wine
  such as Soave

2.5 litres (4 1/2 pints) chicken or
  vegetable stock, kept simmering

400 g (14 oz) Savoy cabbage, finely shredded

1 teaspoon caraway seeds (optional)

120 g (4 1/2 oz) Parmesan cheese, freshly grated

sea salt and freshly milled black pepper

Method

Fry the onion gently in the butter or pork dripping until blond and soft. Add the rice all in one go and toast the grains carefully all over until very dry and shiny but not burned. Add the wine and stir thoroughly. Begin gradually to add the hot stock, one ladleful at a time, stirring constantly. After 10 minutes, add the cabbage and stir very thoroughly, then continue to add stock and stir until the rice is tender. If you like the taste of caraway seeds, stir them into the risotto. Add half the Parmesan and season to taste with salt and pepper. Stir again, cover and leave the risotto to rest for about 3 minutes. Transfer to a warmed serving dish or on to individual warmed plates, sprinkle with the remaining Parmesan and serve.

As an alternative, you can serve the risotto on the cupped outer leaves from the cabbage, which you will have to blanch briefly before using. For a very dramatic effect, serve on blanched red cabbage leaves.

Spinach and Walnut Risotto
Risotto di Spinaci con le Noci

Luganega is a thin, continuous-coil Italian sausage. It is quite coarse in texture and has a fairly strong taste. If you can't get hold of it, use any other kind of raw Italian sausage or half the quantity of finely chopped pancetta.

SERVES 4

600 g (1¼ lb) fresh spinach, washed thoroughly

75 g (3 oz) unsalted butter

150 g (5 oz) *Luganega* or other raw Italian sausage, peeled and crumbled

1 onion, finely chopped

400 g (14 oz) Arborio rice

1 glass dry white wine

1.5 litres (2½ pints) beef or chicken stock, kept simmering

sea salt and freshly milled black pepper

40 g (1½ oz) walnuts, finely chopped

75 g (3 oz) Parmesan cheese, freshly grated

Method

Steam the spinach for a few minutes until soft. Drain very thoroughly, squeeze dry and then chop finely.

Melt half the butter and fry the sausage and onion until the onion is soft and transparent. Add the rice and stir together for a few minutes until the rice grains are well coated in the other ingredients and shining hot. Add the wine and stir together, then add the first ladleful of hot stock, stir and wait for the rice to absorb the liquid. Stir and add more stock only when the previous quantity has been absorbed. Continue to stir and add stock gradually for about 10 minutes until the rice is half cooked. Add the spinach, stir and adjust the seasoning with salt and pepper. Continue to add stock and stir, as before, until the rice is tender and creamy but still firm in the centre of the grains. Remove from the heat, stir in the remaining butter, the walnuts and Parmesan. Cover and leave to rest for 2–3 minutes, then serve immediately on a warmed platter.

Swiss Chard Risotto
Risotto di Bieta

In choosing your chard for this recipe, make sure you buy tender stalks and leaves. As this fantastically wonderful vegetable is only just beginning to be more readily available outside of Italy, you might like to substitute bok choi, which is a similar oriental vegetable. This is one of those risotti which must be served really piping hot.

SERVES 4

1 large mild onion, finely chopped

1 large celery stick, finely chopped

75 g (3 oz) unsalted butter

500 g (1 lb 2 oz) Swiss chard, finely chopped

400 g (14 oz) Arborio rice

1 glass dry white wine

1.5 litres (2½ pints) chicken or vegetable stock, kept simmering

sea salt and freshly milled black pepper

75 g (3 oz) Parmesan cheese, freshly grated, plus extra for serving

Method

Fry the onion and celery very gently in half the butter in a large pan until soft and cooked. Add the chard, stir and add a little water if necessary to cook the chard for a few minutes until completely soft and tender. Add the rice and mix thoroughly until the grains are all shiny, well coated and hot. Pour in the wine, stir and boil for a few minutes until the alcohol has evaporated. Add a little hot stock and stir until the rice has absorbed all the liquid, then add more. Stir, wait for the liquid to vanish, then add more stock. Continue in this way for about 20 minutes until the rice is fluffy and tender but still firm in the centre of the grain. Take the pan off the heat, season with salt and pepper and stir in the remaining butter and the Parmesan. Cover and leave to rest for about 3 minutes, then transfer to a warmed platter and serve immediately. Offer extra Parmesan separately at the table.

Sicilian Risotto
Risotto alla Siciliana

Despite being so far south and therefore many kilometres away from the fog-bound rice fields of Lombardia and Piemonte, the island of Sicily does have a few rice recipes in its repertoire. The most famous of these has to be the ubiquitous *arancini di riso* – deep-fried, orange-shaped rissoles – which are sold in every bar and café throughout the island. I think the rice is here thanks to influences from North Africa rather than from the industrialist north and, as this recipe shows, the interpretation of a risotto is very different on the island.

SERVES 4

1 onion, finely chopped

3 garlic cloves, finely chopped

6 tablespoons extra virgin olive oil

400 g (14 oz) risotto rice

1 glass dry white wine

1.2 litres (2 pints) salted water,
   kept simmering

a handful of black olives,
   stoned and coarsely chopped

1 tablespoon salted capers, rinsed,
   drained and chopped

6 ripe, sweet tomatoes, skinned,
   seeded and coarsely chopped

finely grated zest of 1 lemon

a large pinch of dried oregano

a pinch of dried crushed chilli

sea salt and freshly milled black pepper

Method

Fry the onion and garlic together in half the oil until soft. Stir in the rice and toast the grains thoroughly all over. Pour in the wine and let the rice absorb the liquid and the heat evaporate the alcohol. Now start to cook the rice with boiling water. Add the water gradually, stirring constantly and letting the rice swell with the water before adding any more. After about 20 minutes, when the risotto is creamy but the rice still firm to the bite, stir in the olives, capers, tomatoes, lemon zest, oregano and chilli. Stir through the remaining olive oil and adjust the seasoning to taste. Transfer at once to a warm platter and serve.

Venetian Rice and Peas
Risi e Bisi

This is another recipe which can also be cooked in the old way, without frying the onion in fat at the beginning of the recipe. Like the recipe on page 53, if you choose to make it in this way, the method relies on a slow, rhythmic boil. The end result is really a very thick soup rather than a risotto. Otherwise, you can proceed as with any other risotto, as detailed below, which I think tastes a lot nicer! Try to find pancetta if you can; otherwise you can use top-quality fresh streaky bacon.

SERVES 4

1 kg (2¼ lb) sweet tender young fresh peas
   or 500 g (1 lb 2 oz) frozen petit pois,
   thawed

½ mild, sweet onion, very finely chopped

50 g (2 oz) pancetta, chopped

50 g (2 oz) unsalted butter

3 tablespoons extra virgin olive oil

25 g (1 oz) chopped fresh parsley

1.5 litres (2½ pints) beef, veal or chicken
   stock, kept simmering

300 g (11 oz) risotto rice, preferably Vialone
   Nano Gigante

sea salt and freshly milled black pepper

50 g (2 oz) Parmesan cheese, freshly grated,
   plus extra for serving

Method

If you are using fresh peas, shell them carefully and give them a quick rinse in cold water.

Fry the onion and pancetta in the butter and oil in a heavy-based pan for about 10 minutes. Stir in the parsley and fry gently for a further 4 minutes. Then add the peas and stir thoroughly. Add just enough hot stock barely to cover the ingredients, then simmer very gently until the peas are almost tender, about 15 minutes for fresh or 5 minutes for frozen. Add the rice, stir and add more stock. Season and stir, waiting patiently for the grains to absorb the stock before you add more. After about 20 minutes, when the rice is soft and tender, remove from the heat, stir in the cheese and leave to rest for 3 minutes before turning on to a warmed platter to serve. Offer a little more freshly grated Parmesan at the table.

3 Mushrooms, Herbs and Truffles

I think Mushroom Risotto (page 77) must be one of the most popular of them all. Certainly, it appears to be cooked a great deal and can frequently be found on restaurant menus. This is basically because sweated onion or shallot, butter, rice, mushrooms, stock and Parmesan make a great combination. Using dried porcini gives you the most intense flavour, but there are so many fabulously exotic and different-tasting mushroom varieties readily available that you really should not restrict yourself in any way.

As far as herb risotto goes, I think the combination of rice with really delicious stock and a handful of freshly chopped herbs is something very special indeed. Feel free to experiment with different kinds of fresh herbs, but use a steady hand when it comes to pungent types like rosemary or tarragon.

Truffles and a perfectly-executed risotto were just made for one another. There are only three or four dishes which do justice to the intense, magical flavour of truffles: finely cut, hand-made pasta; soft, white, creamy polenta; fresh, free-range eggs fried in a veritable lake of unsalted butter; and risotto. I have given two versions of how to make a truffle risotto, one using the ancient way of boiling up the rice with the other ingredients, and the other using the more modern method. In either case, the truffle must never be cooked, as it will lose so much of its delicious, earthy, sexy flavour.

Apart from the very best caviar, truffles are the most expensive food there is. Buying and using a truffle is therefore a really special treat, as they cost about the same as gold, weight for weight! A white truffle the size of a walnut, which is about enough to flavour a dish for four people, can set you back as much as £180, depending upon the quality and the time of year. The season is very short, running from late October to early February, and there are good years and very, very bad years. Black truffles, which are not nearly as special as white, cost about half or one-third of the price. Beware of cheap imports (especially of the white truffle) from Romania, Poland and other Balkan states.

Mushroom and Tomato Risotto
Risotto di Funghi al Pomodoro

Passata is a creamy tomato concoction made by puréeing skinned, seeded, canned tomatoes. It is available at all supermarkets and good grocers either in bottles, cans or cartons. It is very convenient as it cooks quickly and gives a smooth, velvety result with little effort.

SERVES 4–6

1 onion, chopped

2 garlic cloves, finely chopped

75 g (3 oz) unsalted butter

1 tablespoon fresh
   rosemary leaves, finely chopped

200 g (7 oz) passata

1 teaspoon concentrated
   tomato purée

1 glass dry white wine

200 g (7 oz) assorted mixed fresh
   mushrooms, sliced

500 g (1 lb 2 oz) Arborio rice

1.5 litres (2½ pints) chicken or
   vegetable stock, kept simmering

sea salt and freshly milled black pepper

freshly grated Parmesan cheese
   for serving

Method

Fry the onion gently with the garlic in half the butter. When the onion is cooked and soft, add the rosemary and passata and stir together, then add the concentrated tomato purée and the wine. Add the mushrooms and cook for a few minutes to let the mushrooms soften a little, then add the rice and stir. Toast the grains until they are shiny and coated and look opaque. Pour in the first ladleful of hot stock and stir until the liquid has evaporated, then add more stock and stir again. Continue to cook the rice in this way for about 20 minutes until it is creamy and smooth, but the rice must still feel firm in the centre of the grain. Remove from the heat, stir in the remaining butter and season to taste with salt and pepper. Cover and leave to rest for 1 minute, then transfer to a warmed platter and serve at once. Offer Parmesan separately at the table.

Mushroom Risotto
Risotto con i Funghi

Time and again this recipe appears to score very highly and many people claim it as their favourite. These days, more exotic varieties of mushroom are being cultivated and are easily available, so you may not even have to go and hunt for them! Of course, for a milder flavour, use ordinary mushrooms.

SERVES 6

200 g (7 oz) mixed wild mushrooms

1 onion, chopped

1–2 garlic cloves, chopped

1 small sprig of fresh rosemary, chopped

100 g (4 oz) unsalted butter

1 large glass dry white wine

500 g (1 lb 2 oz) risotto rice

sea salt and freshly milled black pepper

1.5 litres (2½ pints) chicken or vegetable
   stock, kept simmering

freshly grated Parmesan for serving
   (optional)

Method

Pick over the mushrooms carefully, making sure they are clean and free of any forest debris, then chop them. Put the onion, garlic and rosemary into a large heavy-based pan with half the butter. Fry gently together until the onion is soft. Add the chopped mushrooms and stir together thoroughly. Cook the mushrooms until just soft. Add the wine, stir and wait for the alcohol to boil off. Stir in the rice and heat through until hot and shining, season with salt and pepper, then begin the cooking process, adding a little hot stock at a time and waiting for the rice to absorb it, stirring thoroughly each time you add more liquid. Continue in this way for about 20 minutes until the rice is tender and all the grains are plump and fluffy. Remove from the heat and stir in the remaining butter. Cover and leave to stand for about 3 minutes before transferring to a warmed platter to serve. You can offer Parmesan cheese separately, but if the mushrooms are really full of flavour, the Parmesan is unnecessary.

Genoese Risotto
Risotto alla Genovese

A most unusual cooking method is used for this recipe, but the final result is delicious. Pecorino is a hard cheese, similar to Parmesan, but made from sheeps' milk.

SERVES 6

1 onion, chopped

4 tablespoons extra virgin olive oil

100 g (4 oz) fresh mushrooms, sliced

250 g (9 oz) canned chopped tomatoes

sea salt and freshly milled black pepper

1.5 litres (2½ pints) water

500 g (1 lb 2 oz) risotto rice

6 tablespoons freshly grated Parmesan
   or Pecorino cheese

Method

Fry the onion gently in the oil until soft. Stir in the mushrooms and cook together for about 5 minutes. Add the tomatoes, season to taste with salt and pepper and cover.

In a separate pan, bring the water to the boil with a large pinch of salt. Add the rice and stir, return to the boil, then boil for 5 minutes. Drain well, reserving the cooking water, and add the rice to the pan with the tomatoes and mushrooms. Stir the rice carefully and finish off cooking by adding the rice water a ladleful at a time, stirring and waiting for the rice to absorb the water before adding any more. Season to taste with salt and pepper and continue to cook for about 15 minutes until the risotto is creamy but the rice very firm in the centre of the grains. Stir in the cheese, cook for a further few minutes and then transfer to a warmed dish to serve.

Traditional Truffle Risotto
Risotto al Tartufo Classico

This is a recipe which is very old indeed, and therefore the cooking technique is different to that used for most of the other recipes contained in this collection. Unlike other risotto recipes, the rice is cooked in the stock, which must be as rich and dense as possible.

SERVES 4

40 g (1 ½ oz) pork fat

40 g (1 ½ oz) fat and lean
  prosciutto crudo

1 onion, chopped

1 carrot, thinly sliced

1 celery stick, chopped

400 g (14 oz) beef skirt, chuck
  or similar, cut into large chunks

1. 5 litres (2 ½ pints) boiling water

sea salt and freshly milled black pepper

400 g (14 oz) risotto rice

75 g (3 oz) unsalted butter

75 g (3 oz) Parmesan cheese,
  freshly grated

freshly shaved white truffle,
  to taste and affordability

Method

Begin by chopping the pork fat, prosciutto and onion together to make a thick paste. Place this in the bottom of a heavy stock pot and fry together until the onion is soft and golden. Add the carrot and celery and fry together for about 5 minutes, then add all the beef and brown it thoroughly on all sides. Cover with the boiling water, season with salt and pepper and place a lid on the pot. Leave to simmer gently for about 3 hours.

Remove the meat from the stock and discard it. Put the stock and all that remains in it through a food mill, then return it to the pan and bring to a slow boil. You should have about 1.2 litres (2½ pints). Add in all the rice, stir and simmer for about 20 minutes until the grains are all plump, fluffy and tender and all the liquid has been absorbed. Add the butter and Parmesan, stir together thoroughly. Cover and leave to stand for 5 minutes, then turn out on to a warmed serving platter. While the risotto is resting, make sure the truffle is clean and ready to use. Cover the risotto liberally with freshly shaved truffle and serve at once.

Truffle Risotto
Risotto al Tartufo

The best white truffles come from the little town of Alba in Piedmont. If you visit Alba during truffle season, transport your unwrapped truffles home in a jar of risotto rice. The rice will become lightly infused and can be used to make truffle-flavoured risotto. Alternatively, seek out truffles through your favourite Italian restaurant. They may get them in for customers or know a ready source.

If you have no truffle, use half the amount of butter at the beginning and stir a few spoonfuls of truffle oil into the risotto at the end when you add the cheese. Arneis is a very intensely flavoured, dry white wine, so much so that in its native Piedmont it is often used to marinate and cook game.

SERVES 4–6

100 g (4 oz) unsalted butter

3 shallots, finely chopped

500 g (1 lb 2 oz) risotto rice, preferably Carnaroli

½ bottle full bodied dry white wine such as Arneis

1 litre (1¾ pints) chicken or vegetable stock, kept simmering

sea salt and freshly milled black pepper

50 g (2 oz) Parmesan cheese, freshly grated

1 white or black truffle, cleaned, or 2–3 tablespoons truffle oil

Method

Melt half the butter and fry the shallots gently until soft and transparent. Add the rice and stir until shiny and coated with melted butter, but not coloured. Pour over the wine and stir until the alcohol has evaporated and the rice has absorbed all the liquid, then begin to stir in the hot stock, one ladleful at a time. Continue adding stock, stirring and waiting for the rice to absorb the liquid, then adding more stock. Season to taste with salt and pepper. When the rice is creamy and tender, though still firm in the centre of the grains, remove from the heat. Stir in the remaining butter and the Parmesan. Cover and leave the risotto to rest for 2 minutes, then transfer to a warmed platter, shave over the truffle and serve at once.

Rocket Risotto
Risotto Alla Rucola

I adore the taste of rocket so much I could not leave it out of this collection of recipes. Be sure only to let the rocket wilt but not actually cook as this alters the flavour.

SERVES 4

1 onion, chopped

75 g (3 oz) unsalted butter

400 g (14 oz) risotto rice

½ glass dry white wine

1.2 litres (2 pints) chicken stock, kept simmering

2 handful-sized bunches of rocket, coarsely chopped

3 tablespoons single cream

50 g (2 oz) Parmesan cheese, freshly grated

sea salt and freshly milled black pepper

Method

Fry the onion gently in half the butter until soft. Add the rice and toast it thoroughly all over until it is sizzling hot and opaque. Add the wine and boil for a minute to evaporate the alcohol. Begin to add the hot stock, a ladleful at a time, stirring constantly and making sure the rice absorbs all the liquid before adding any more. Gradually, as you stir and add liquid, the risotto will become more creamy and smooth. After about 20 minutes, when the risotto is ready, in other words velvety and rippling but with the grains still holding their shape and feeling firm to the bite, stir in the remaining butter, the rocket, cream and Parmesan. Adjust the seasoning, stir again and cover. Leave to rest for 2 minutes, then transfer to a warmed platter and serve at once.

Tomato and Basil Risotto
Risotto con Pomodori e Basilico

This is a recipe from Liguria, so do use the appropriate olive oil if you can to make it really authentic. If the tomato skins are very tough, it would be a good idea to skin the tomatoes first. To do this easily, nick the skins carefully, (you only need a very small nick) plunge them into boiling water for one minute, then drain, dry and take the skins off with a sharp knife.

SERVES 6

a handful of fresh basil leaves

2 garlic cloves, chopped

6 ripe, squashy tomatoes, coarsely chopped

120 ml (4 fl oz) extra virgin olive oil,
   preferably Ligurian

sea salt and freshly milled black pepper

150 g (5 oz) pine nuts

600 g (1 1/4 lb) Arborio rice

1 large glass dry white wine

1.5 litres (2 1/2 pints) vegetable stock, kept
   simmering

75 g (3 oz) Pecorino or Parmesan cheese,
   freshly grated

Method

Put the basil, garlic and tomatoes in a pan with half the oil and fry gently together for about 10 minutes to form a thick, chunky sauce. Season with salt and pepper and when the sauce is glossy, take it off the heat and leave to one side until required.

Meanwhile, pour the rest of the oil into a second pan, add the pine nuts and toast until golden but not dark brown. Add the rice and toast it in the same way. Then add the wine and stir until the alcohol has evaporated. Now begin gradually to add the hot stock and stir the rice as it absorbs the liquid. Remember to do this at the pace of the rice; in other words, keep stirring gently and never add more stock than the rice can take at one time. About half way through this process, after about 10 minutes, add the tomato, basil and garlic sauce. Stir and resume the cooking process with the hot stock as before. When the grains are still firm in the middle but the risotto is creamy and velvety, take it off the heat and stir in the Pecorino or Parmesan. Cover and leave to rest for 2 minutes, then transfer to a warmed platter and serve at once.

Pesto Risotto
Risotto al Pesto

I like to make this risotto especially creamy and then – for contrast – I finish it off with finely chopped fresh basil and a few toasted pine nuts. The simplest way to toast pine nuts is to shake them over a medium heat in a dry pan until just golden.

SERVES 4

1 onion, finely chopped

1 garlic clove, finely chopped

4 tablespoons extra virgin olive oil

400 g (14 oz) risotto rice

1.2 litres (2 pints) chicken or vegetable
   stock, kept simmering

3 tablespoons good quality pesto

sea salt and freshly milled black pepper

3 tablespoons double cream or 2 tablespoons
   Mascarpone cheese

4 tablespoons freshly grated Parmesan cheese

a handful of fresh basil leaves, chopped

a handful of pine nuts, lightly toasted

Method

Fry the onion and garlic gently in the olive oil until the onion is soft, then add the rice. Raise the heat and stir the rice thoroughly until well toasted. Add the first ladleful of hot stock and stir until the rice has absorbed the liquid. Add more stock, stir again and repeat the process for about 20 minutes until the risotto is velvety but the grains are still firm in the middle. Stir in the pesto and heat through. Season to taste with salt and pepper, then remove from the heat. Stir in the cream or Mascarpone and the Parmesan. Cover and leave to rest for 2–3 minutes, then stir once more and transfer to a warmed platter. Sprinkle with the basil and the pine nuts and serve at once.

Garlic Risotto
Risotto all'Aglio

Another Ligurian recipe, you can vary the amount of garlic you use for this recipe according to taste and circumstance.

SERVES 4

5 garlic cloves, finely chopped

a large handful of fresh flatleaf parsley, stalks
  discarded and leaves finely chopped

75 ml (3 fl oz) extra virgin olive oil,
  preferably Ligurian

sea salt and freshly milled black pepper

100 g (4 oz) canned tomatoes, drained

75 g (3 oz) cooked ham, coarsely chopped

500 g (1 lb 2 oz) Arborio rice

1.5 litres (2¹/₂ pints) vegetable stock,
  kept simmering

50 g (2 oz) Parmesan cheese, freshly grated,
  plus extra for serving

Method

Fry the garlic and parsley gently in the oil for about 5 minutes or until the garlic is softened. Season thoroughly with salt and pepper and add the tomatoes and ham. Stir them around to break them up and when they are hot and bubbling, add the rice and stir. When the rice is hot and well covered with the other ingredients, begin to add the hot stock. Stir and add stock gradually, waiting for the rice to absorb the liquid before adding more. Continue in this way for about 20 minutes until the rice is tender and creamy but still firm in the centre of the grains. Remove from the heat, stir in the Parmesan, cover and leave to rest for 1 minute. Transfer to a warmed platter and serve at once. Offer extra Parmesan separately at the table.

Parsley Risotto
Risotto di Prezzemolo

This is possibly my favourite risotto of them all as it essentially encompasses my philosophy of food: less is more! In other words, all the best recipes are those which use very few ingredients of the best possible quality, then do as little as possible to them. You must use flatleaf parsley for this risotto. I have tried to make the same recipe with the curly variety, but with disappointing results. Pinot Grigio is my preference for a suitable wine.

SERVES 4

1 onion, very finely chopped

75 g (3 oz) unsalted butter

400 g (14 oz) Arborio rice

1 glass dry white wine

1.5 litres (2½ pints) chicken stock, kept simmering

sea salt and freshly milled black pepper

a huge bunch of fresh flatleaf parsley, stalks discarded
   and leaves finely chopped

75 g (3 oz) Parmesan cheese, freshly grated

Method

Fry the onion gently in half the butter until soft and transparent. Add the rice and turn the grains over in the butter and onion until coated and shiny. Add the wine and stir thoroughly. After 1 minute, add the first ladleful of hot stock. Stir and allow the liquid to vanish, then add the next ladleful. Wait for the grains to absorb the stock, stirring gently, then add more stock. Continue in this way for about 20 minutes until the rice is soft, tender and creamy, but the grains must remain firm in the centre. Season with salt and pepper and remove from the heat. Stir in the rest of the butter, the parsley and the Parmesan. Stir thoroughly and cover. Leave the risotto to rest for 2 minutes, then transfer to a warmed platter and serve at once.

Saffron Risotto
Risotto allo Zafferano

This is really a different version of a Milanese risotto, but unlike the classic recipe on page 121 it contains no bone marrow and it does contain a glass of wine. You can add more saffron if you want a brighter colour and a more intense flavour. I like to make the recipe with chicken stock, but you can use beef stock if you prefer.

SERVES 6

1 onion, finely chopped

100 g (4 oz) unsalted butter

500 g (1 lb 2 oz) risotto rice

1 glass dry white wine

1.5 litres (2½ pints) chicken or beef stock, kept simmering

1–3 sachets of saffron powder

75 g (3 oz) Parmesan cheese, freshly grated

sea salt and freshly milled black pepper

Method

Fry the onion very gently in half the butter until soft and shiny. Pour in the rice and stir it around until the grains are opaque and very hot without browning. Pour over the wine and stir until the liquid has been absorbed and the alcohol evaporated. Add the first ladleful of hot stock, stir and wait for it to be absorbed, then add more stock and repeat. Continue in this way, always waiting for the rice to swell with the stock it has absorbed before adding more. You should keep a constant ripple going in the pot – never too wet and never dried out for more than a few seconds. About half way through, after 10 minutes, stir the saffron through the rice, then continue to add the stock. When the risotto is velvety and creamy, but with each grain still firm to the bite in the middle, take it off the heat and stir in the remaining butter and the Parmesan. Adjust the seasoning and cover. Leave to rest for about 3 minutes, then transfer to a warmed serving platter and serve immediately.

Nettle Risotto
Risotto all'Ortica

If you ever make anything at all with nettles, make sure you are wearing a really good, stout pair of gloves before you even consider going out to start picking. Any nettle recipe, be it risotto, pasta, soup or salad, calls ideally for those lovely, fresh, tender, soft green sprigs which you will find in the spring. Should you opt to make this dish with older nettles, they must be stripped down to the stalk to remove their strings or the results may be a little chewy! Basically, you should treat nettles like most other green, leafy vegetables.

SERVES 4

1 large mild, onion, finely chopped

1 large celery stick, finely chopped

75 g (3 oz) unsalted butter

500 g (1 lb 2 oz) freshly picked nettles, thoroughly washed and dried, then finely chopped

400 g (14 oz) Arborio rice

1 glass medium dry white or rosé wine

1.5 litres (2½ pints) chicken or vegetable stock, kept simmering

75 g (3 oz) Parmesan cheese, freshly grated, plus extra for serving

sea salt and freshly milled black pepper

Method

Fry the onion and celery in half the butter until soft. Add the nettles and stir, then cook for a few minutes until completely soft and tender, adding a little water if necessary. Add the rice and mix thoroughly until the grains are all shiny, well coated and hot. Pour in the wine and stir to evaporate. Add a little hot stock and stir until the rice has absorbed all the liquid, then add more. Stir, wait for the liquid to be absorbed, then add more stock. Continue in this way for about 20 minutes until the rice is fluffy and tender but still firm in the centre of the grain. Remove from the heat and stir in the remaining butter and the Parmesan. Season with salt and pepper. Cover and leave to rest for about 3 minutes, then transfer to a warmed platter and serve immediately. Offer extra Parmesan separately at the table.

4 Fish and Seafood

There is only one word I want to say about the subject of this chapter and that is FRESHNESS! The difference in flavour between tired fish and fresh fish is like the difference between night and day, and you should always insist on never cooking fish that is not as fresh as it can possibly be. That's without even mentioning the health risks of less-than-fresh seafood, especially shellfish and molluscs.

My favourite recipe in this chapter is the one created by my mother, Fiammetta, which appears on page 110. This incredibly simple yet very sophisticated dish was the sort of meal she would serve for a family supper every once in a while when I was a little girl. As I have always had an over-powering passion for mussels, this was one dish that was always going to be popular with me! Looking back, it was quite a brave and enlightened idea to serve this without any qualms to a young family – I mean it is hardly fish fingers . . . but then I never saw a fish finger until I came to London in the very late 1970s.

The recipe which might cause you a problem – though I sincerely hope it does not – is the Eel Risotto on page 99. I know eels can be hard to find, difficult to prepare and not to everybody's liking, so I have proposed that you use smoked eel fillets instead. This will not give you quite the same results but it still makes a fabulous dish. I have a memory of an eel risotto which I ate near Treviso while making my television series – it still manages to make my mouth water! Just thinking about it transports me back to the simple riverside trattoria where it was made and served, and this too is a little piece of heaven.

Salmon Risotto
Risotto al Salmone

SERVES 4

400 g (14 oz) salmon tail fillet

I bay leaf

sea salt

5 black peppercorns

grated rind of ½ lemon

a handful of fresh parsley

I garlic clove, chopped

75 g (3 oz) unsalted butter

I tablespoon olive oil

400 g (14 oz) risotto rice, preferably
   Vialone Nano

I glass dry white wine

2 tablespoons finely chopped fresh parsley

finely grated zest of I very small lemon

2 slices smoked salmon, cut into fine strips

Method

Wash and check over the fish, removing any visible bones. Place the bay leaf, salt, peppercorns, lemon zest and parsley in a pan large enough to hold the fish and cover with water. Bring to the boil, then simmer gently for about 20 minutes. Lower the salmon into the water and poach for about 10 minutes, then cover and remove from the heat. Leave the salmon to stand in the hot stock until cooked through. Remove the fish from the stock, skin and fillet carefully, then cut into small pieces. Strain the stock, return it to a pan and keep it simmering.

Fry the garlic with half the butter and the oil in a deep, heavy-based pan until just softened. Add the rice and toast the grains thoroughly, then add the wine and cook for 2–3 minutes to allow the alcohol to burn off. Begin to add the hot salmon stock, stirring constantly and always allowing the liquid to be absorbed before adding more. After about 15 minutes, stir in the cooked fish fillets, breaking some up as you stir them through, then continue adding the stock. When the rice is tender, take the pan off the heat and stir in the remaining butter. Cover and leave to rest for 2 minutes, then transfer to a warmed platter. Sprinkle with the chopped parsley, lemon zest and the tiny strips of smoked salmon to serve.

Whiting Risotto
Risotto al Nasello

Whiting is now quite easy to find in fishmongers and supermarkets. It has a delicate flavour and its flesh will fall apart more easily for a better result in this risotto, although if it proves elusive you can use cod instead.

SERVES 4

400 g (14 oz) whiting fillets

2 tablespoons plain white flour

100 g (4 oz) unsalted butter

2 glasses dry white wine

sea salt and freshly milled black pepper

1 onion, finely chopped

400 g (14 oz) Arborio rice

1.5 litres (2½ pints) fish stock, kept simmering

3 tablespoons finely chopped fresh flatleaf parsley

Method

Coat the fish lightly in the flour. Melt half the butter in a frying pan and quickly fry the fish for a few minutes until cooked. Add about a quarter of the wine and boil quickly to evaporate the alcohol. Season with salt and pepper and leave to one side.

Melt the remaining butter in a separate pan and fry the onion gently until soft and transparent. Add the rice and stir to coat the grains thoroughly with butter and onion. When the rice is crackling hot, add the rest of the wine and boil off the alcohol for a couple of minutes. Then proceed to cook the rice by adding one ladleful of hot stock at a time and stirring. Always wait for the rice to absorb the liquid before adding more. After about 15 minutes, when the rice is about three-quarters cooked, add the fish fillets and stir through, breaking up the fish a little. Continue to add stock and stir gently until the rice is cooked but still firm in the centre. Remove from the heat, stir in the parsley and plenty of freshly milled black pepper, cover and leave to rest for 1 minute. Transfer to a warmed platter and serve at once.

Mackerel and Rosemary Risotto
Risotto allo Sgombro con Rosmarino

This is such a delicious and highly under-rated fish, I feel it must have a place in this collection. The perfect herb partner for mackerel has, in my opinion, always been rosemary.

SERVES 4

1 large or 2 small mackerel, gutted and cleaned

6 tablespoons extra virgin olive oil

3 garlic cloves, finely chopped

1 large sprig of fresh rosemary (about 10 cm/4 in)

sea salt and freshly milled black pepper

2 glasses dry white wine

1.2 litres (2 pints) fish stock, kept simmering

400 g (14 oz) Arborio rice

Method

Preheat the oven to 190°C/375°F/gas mark 5.

Slash the skin of the fish in three or four places on either side. Oil an oven-proof dish thoroughly with some of the oil and lay the fish in the dish. Push some of the garlic into the slits, leaving about half the amount for the rice. Tear about half the leaves off the rosemary and push these leaves into the slits. Season the fish thoroughly inside and out, then pour 1 glass of wine over the fish. Bake for about 20 minutes until flaky and cooked through. Leave to cool, then skin, fillet and flake the fish roughly. Put the juices from the pan through a sieve and reserve. Add the skin, bones and head of the fish to the simmering stock to add extra flavour.

Chop the rest of the rosemary leaves very finely and fry them with the reserved garlic in the remaining olive oil for about 2 minutes. Add the rice and turn it quickly to coat it with oil, garlic and rosemary. When the rice is very hot but not browned, add the second glass of wine and the juices from the pan in which the mackerel was baked. Stir until the alcohol has evaporated. Now begin gradually to add the hot stock (straining off the skin and bones), stirring after each addition and waiting for the grains to absorb the stock before adding more liquid. After 10 minutes, about half way through the cooking time, season to taste with salt and pepper and add the flaked mackerel. Stir through and continue the cooking process as before. When the risotto is velvety and creamy, transfer to a warmed platter and serve at once.

Tuna Risotto
Risotto al Tonno

Italian canned tuna is far superior to any other, so please try to buy a brand like Palmera or Rio Mare if you can. Also, make sure the tuna is canned in olive oil.

SERVES 4

1 large onion, finely chopped

120 g (4$^{1}/_{2}$ oz) unsalted butter

500 g (1 lb 2 oz) Arborio rice

1 glass dry white wine

1.5 litres (2$^{1}/_{2}$ pints) vegetable stock, kept simmering

sea salt and freshly milled black pepper

2 tablespoons plain white flour

500 ml (17 fl oz) milk

120 g (4$^{1}/_{2}$ oz) canned tuna in olive oil, drained and flaked

4 tablespoons finely chopped fresh parsley

Method

Fry the onion gently in one-third of the butter until soft and shiny. Add the rice and stir to cover it thoroughly in butter and onion. When the rice is opaque and very hot but not browned, add the glass of wine and let the alcohol evaporate, then begin to add the hot stock. Add it gradually, stirring after each addition and making sure all the liquid has been absorbed before adding any more. Season with salt and pepper to taste.

Meanwhile, melt the remaining butter in a separate pan until foaming but not brown. Add the flour and stir to a paste. Add the milk and whisk energetically to prevent any lumps. Season with salt and pepper, then simmer gently for about 10 minutes or until quite thick and with no taste of flour, stirring continously. Add the flaked tuna and the parsley, stir and remove from the heat. When the risotto is creamy and velvety but still with firm grains, transfer it to a warmed platter. Pour the tuna sauce over the rice and serve at once.

Sardine and Tomato Risotto
Risotto di Sardine al Pomodoro

Try to buy sardines as fresh as possible. Sardines which are cooked within hours of catching tend to stay much firmer and hold their shape and texture very well. If they do break up during cooking, don't worry too much as you'll still get all the flavour if not the texture.

SERVES 4

2 garlic cloves, finely chopped

400 g (14 oz) gutted, headless, filleted sardines

4 tablespoons extra virgin olive oil

6 ripe, squashy tomatoes, skinned and coarsely chopped

400 g (14 oz) Arborio rice

1 glass dry white wine

1 teaspoon lemon juice

1.2 litres (2 pints) fish stock, kept simmering

sea salt and freshly milled black pepper

3 tablespoons chopped fresh parsley

Method

Fry the garlic and sardines in the oil for about 5 minutes until the sardines are half cooked. Remove and discard their tails as they become loose and break up the sardines a little. Add the tomatoes and stir until the fish, garlic and tomatoes have all heated through and are mixed together roughly. Add the rice and pour over the wine and lemon juice. Boil for 2 minutes to evaporate the alcohol, then add the first ladleful of hot stock. Stir and allow the rice to absorb the liquid, then add more. Continue in this way until the rice is creamy and velvety but still firm in the centre of the grains. Add salt and pepper to taste, then add the parsley, stir once more and transfer to a warmed platter to serve at once.

Anchovy and Tomato Risotto
Risotto alle Acciughe e Pomodoro

This recipe is unusual for risotto in that you will not need stock. This is because the very powerful flavour of the anchovies means you only need boiling water. If the tomato purée is a bit insipid, use fewer anchovies. It really is best to use salted anchovies rather than those canned in oil as they have a better flavour. You can buy them in delicatessens.

SERVES 6

2 large onions, chopped

4 tablespoons extra virgin olive oil

12 salted anchovies, washed, boned and dried

4 tablespoons concentrated tomato purée

4 tablespoons chopped fresh flatleaf parsley

1 fresh sage leaf

600 g (1 1/4 lb) Arborio rice

1 large glass dry white wine

1.5 litres (2 1/2 pints) water, kept simmering

sea salt and freshly milled black pepper

50 g (2 oz) Pecorino cheese, freshly grated

Method

Fry the onions very gently in the olive oil until they are completely soft and translucent. Add a little water to them as they cook to prevent them from caramelizing. When they are cooked, add the anchovies and stir vigorously together so that the anchovies blend into the onions. Add the tomato purée and mix thoroughly. Add a little water to make a thick sauce texture and stir in the parsley and sage. Cover and leave to simmer for about 15 minutes, stirring occasionally.

Add the rice and stir for a few minutes until the rice is well coated and crackling hot. Add the wine and stir for 1 minute, then begin the cooking process using boiling water. Stir in a ladleful of hot water, stir and wait for the water to be absorbed, then add another. Continue for about 20 minutes until the rice is tender and fluffy. Check the seasoning; you may not need any more salt as the anchovies tend to be very salty. Add pepper to taste. At the end of the cooking time, take the risotto off the heat and stir in the Pecorino. Cover and leave to rest for 2–3 minutes, then transfer to a warmed platter and serve at once.

Eel Risotto
Risotto con l'Anguilla

When I was a child, we used to fish for eels in the ditches around our home, using upturned umbrellas into which our catch would swim and become ensnared. The eels would then be kept in clean, fresh water, which was scrupulously changed twice a day for a whole month before they were considered fit for human consumption. We would then sell them to nearby restaurants for pocket money. Considering where eels like to live, when you catch or buy your eel, please be sure it has been carefully cleaned. Also, be aware that an eel doesn't keep, so as soon as you have got it home, it will need to be cooked. You can adapt this recipe for another fish, such as smoked eel fillets, for a slightly different flavour.

SERVES 4

I x 600 g (1 1/4 lb) fresh eel

3 garlic cloves, chopped

I onion, chopped

I bay leaf

3 tablespoons extra virgin olive oil

75 g (3 oz) unsalted butter

1.25 litres (2 1/2 pints) light fish stock, kept simmering

400 g (14 oz) Arborio rice

sea salt and freshly milled black pepper

Method

Clean the eel very carefully and cut it into large chunks. Do not skin the eel. Fry the garlic, onion and bay leaf with the oil and half the butter until the onion is softened. Add the eel and continue to cook gently, basting with a little of the fish stock so that the eel is submerged but not drowning. When the eel is very tender (the cooking time will depend on the thickness of the eel), take it out of the pan and carefully remove all the flesh. Discard the bones and skin. Strain the contents of the pan into a clean pan and return to a simmer. Add the rice and stir until the rice has absorbed all the liquid, then return the eel to the pan and stir. Continue to cook the rice, adding a ladleful of stock, stirring until the rice has absorbed the liquid, then adding more stock and repeating the process. Carry on for about 20 minutes until the rice is tender and the texture velvety but make sure the rice grains are still firm to the bite. Take the risotto off the heat, stir in the remaining butter and season with salt and pepper. Cover and leave the risotto to rest for 2 minutes, then transfer to a warmed platter and serve at once.

Scallop Risotto
Risotto di Capesante

If possible, buy fresh scallops rather than frozen and go for the smaller, sweeter specimens rather than the huge ones. Please be very careful not to overcook scallops or they really will be like rubber bands.

SERVES 6

1.5 kg (3 lb) scallops in their shells, cleaned

100 g (4 oz) unsalted butter

4 tablespoons brandy

sea salt and freshly milled black pepper

3 shallots, finely chopped

500 g (1 lb 2 oz) risotto rice, preferably Carnaroli

1.5 litres (2½ pints) fish stock, kept simmering

2 tablespoons finely chopped fresh flatleaf parsley

3 tablespoons double cream

Method

Clean the scallops and discard the shells. Remove the corals from the rest of the flesh. If the scallops are very big, cut them in half. Heat half the butter and quickly fry the scallops on either side for 2–3 minutes. Pour over the brandy and light it by tipping the pan to catch the gas flame or lighting it with a taper. Let the flames die down, then season and remove from the heat. Reserve until required.

Meanwhile heat the remaining butter in a separate pan and fry the shallots gently until soft. Add the rice and mix together until the rice is crackling hot and shiny. Pour in the first ladleful of hot stock. Stir and allow the grains to absorb the liquid, then add some more and repeat. Continue in this way for about 15 minutes or until the rice is about three-quarters cooked. Now add the cooked scallops and all their juices, the corals and the parsley. Stir together and resume the cooking process as before. When the risotto is creamy and velvety but the grains are still firm to the bite, take it off the heat. Stir in the cream, cover and leave to rest for about 2 minutes. Transfer to a warmed platter and serve at once.

Prawn Risotto
Risotto di Gamberetti

I know the prawn butter seems like a huge taradiddle, but it is actually quite fun to do and really is worth the trouble.

SERVES 4–6

200 g (7 oz) unsalted butter

1 carrot, finely chopped

1 onion, chopped

6 fresh parsley stalks, chopped

½ bay leaf

750 g (1¾ lb) raw, shell-on prawns

½ glass brandy

a bowl of iced water

3 tablespoons extra virgin olive oil

500 g (1 lb 2 oz) risotto rice,
    preferably Carnaroli

2 glasses dry white wine

1.5 litres (2½ pints) fish stock,
    kept simmering

sea salt and freshly milled black pepper

freshly grated Parmesan cheese
    for serving

Method

Fry together 40 g (1½ oz) of the butter, the carrot, half the onion, the parsley and the bay leaf until soft. Add the prawns and cook them quickly, basting with the brandy for a few minutes until they turn pink. Take the pan off the heat and lift out the prawns. Remove the heads and peel the tails, reserving them separately.

Next, make the prawn butter. Take all the shells, heads and vegetables from cooking the prawns. Put them all in a food processor and process until completely smooth. Melt the 120 g (4½ oz) of the butter very gently in a pan. Add the prawn purée and mix together thoroughly until you have formed a thick paste. Spoon this mixture into a clean napkin. Squeeze the napkin tightly to let the melted butter fall through the cloth into the bowl of iced water. It will collect together almost immediately and rise to the surface. When you have squeezed everything out, discard the contents of the napkin and leave the butter to form a skin on the water, then remove with a slotted spoon and set to one side.

Fry the rest of the onion in the remaining butter and the oil until soft and transparent. Add the rice and stir until hot and shiny, then pour in the wine and boil for 1 minute until the alcohol has evaporated. Begin to add hot stock to the rice, stirring and adding stock gradually once the rice has absorbed the previous addition of stock. Continue in this way for about 20 minutes until the rice is cooked, velvety and creamy but still firm in the centre of the grain. Adjust the seasoning to taste. Remove from the heat and stir in the prawn butter and the prawn tails. Cover and leave to rest for 2 minutes, then stir once more and transfer to a warmed platter to serve at once with the Parmesan served separately.

Quick Prawn Risotto
Risotto di Gamberi Velocissimo

SERVES 4

1 onion, very finely chopped

1/4 celery stick, very finely chopped

75 g (3 oz) unsalted butter

400 g (14 oz) Arborio rice

1/2 bottle dry white wine such
   as Pinot Grigio

1 litre (1 3/4 pints) chicken or vegetable
   stock, kept simmering

450 g (1 lb) cooked, peeled prawns

50 g (2 oz) Parmesan cheese, freshly grated

2 tablespoons chopped fresh flatleaf parsley

sea salt and freshly milled black pepper

Method

Fry the onion and celery gently in half the butter until soft and translucent. Stir in the rice and heat until opaque and crackling hot. Stir in a glass of wine and heat for 1 minute until the alcohol has evaporated, then add continue to add all the wine in this way. Stir in the first ladleful of hot stock, allowing the rice to absorb the stock before adding more. Continue adding the stock a ladleful at a time until you have added almost all the stock, then stir in the prawns so they have time just to heat through while you finish the cooking. After about 20 minutes, when the risotto is creamy but the rice is still firm to the bite, remove from the heat and stir in the remaining butter, the Parmesan and the parsley. Adjust the seasoning, cover and leave to rest for 2 minutes. Stir once more, then transfer to a warmed platter to serve.

Brown Shrimp Risotto
Risotto di Gamberetti Bruni

The taste of freshly boiled, sweet little brown shrimps will always remind me of tea time in Norfolk. When I lived there, the Saturday trip to Swaffham market was obligatory and, depending on the season, I usually came back with a couple of pints of these delicious, tiny shrimps. They are a real bind to peel, but well worth all the effort. I used to serve them for tea with very finely sliced brown bread and butter because it made my mother nostalgic for her years in Brussels. So I dedicate this dish to my Belgian grandmother, after whom I am named. Incidentally, if you wish, you can use the shells from these shrimps to make butter as described on page 102. Be careful, however, as they can be rather salty, so rinse the shrimps well before shelling them.

SERVES 4–6

100 g (4 oz) unsalted butter

1 carrot, finely chopped

1 onion, chopped

6 fresh parsley stalks, chopped

$\frac{1}{2}$ bay leaf

750 g (1$\frac{3}{4}$ lb) cooked peeled
  brown shrimps

1 large glass dry white wine

500 g (1 lb 2 oz) risotto rice

1.5 litres (2$\frac{1}{2}$ pints) fish stock,
  kept simmering

sea salt and freshly milled black pepper

3 tablespoons double cream

1 tablespoon finely snipped
  fresh chives

Method

Fry the butter, carrot, onion, parsley and bay leaf until the vegetables are soft. Discard the bay leaf and add the shrimps, turning them quickly and basting with the wine until they are heated through. Add the rice and stir until shiny, then pour in the first ladleful of hot stock. When the stock has been absorbed, add more stock to the rice, stirring and adding more stock gradually each time the rice has absorbed the previous addition of liquid. Continue in this way for about 20 minutes until the rice is cooked, velvety and creamy but still firm in the centre of the grain. Adjust the seasoning and stir in the cream. Cover and leave to rest for 2 minutes, then stir again, adding the chives. Transfer to a warmed platter and serve at once.

Mussel Risotto
Risotto con le Cozze

SERVES 4

1.25 kg (2³/₄ lb) fresh, live mussels,
 scrubbed and thoroughly cleaned

600 g (1¹/₄ lb) ripe, squashy tomatoes

2 garlic cloves, finely chopped

6 tablespoons extra virgin olive oil

500 g (1 lb 2 oz) Arborio rice

1.2 litres (2 pints) fish stock, kept simmering

a handful of fresh flatleaf parsley,
 finely chopped

sea salt and freshly milled black pepper

25 g (1 oz) unsalted butter

Method

Put all the clean mussels into a wide, shallow pan, discarding any which are not closed or do not close when tapped sharply. Put a lid on the pan and put the pan over a medium to high heat. Shake the pan over the heat, encouraging all the mussels to open up. After about 8 minutes, all those which are going to open will have done so. Discard any which remain closed. Take out the mussels as they open. Remove the mussels from the shells and discard all but the prettiest shells which you can save for garnish. Strain the liquid from the mussels through a very fine sieve. Under no circumstances force open a mussel that has not opened after cooking.

Next, push the fresh, squashy tomatoes through a sieve or food mill. Now fry the garlic and oil together until the garlic is blond, then add all the rice. Mix together thoroughly until the rice is crackling hot and well coated in oil and garlic. Now add the liquid from the mussels with the strained tomatoes. Mix together until the rice has absorbed the liquid, then begin gradually to add the hot fish stock. Stir constantly and only add more stock when the previous amount has been absorbed by the rice. Continue in this way for about 10 minutes until the rice is half cooked, then add the mussels and the parsley. Season with salt and pepper and resume adding stock, stirring and adding more stock once the rice has soaked up the previous stock. When the rice is creamy and velvety but the grains are still firm in the centre, take the risotto off the heat and stir in the butter. Cover and leave to rest for 1 minute, then transfer to a warmed platter, decorate with the reserved shells and serve at once.

Lobster Risotto
Risotto all'Aragosta

Although it isn't vital, having a pestle and mortar is important if the lobster stock is to be really flavoursome. Without the rich lobster stock you will get a much blander flavour. For a crab risotto, proceed in exactly the same way. You will probably need three very large crabs to get the same amount of meat.

SERVES 4–6

2 medium-sized boiled lobsters, halved

100 g (4 oz) unsalted butter

1 celery stick, coarsely chopped

1 carrot, coarsely chopped

1 onion, coarsely chopped

a handful of fresh flatleaf parsley, coarsely chopped

1 sprig of fresh tarragon

4 tablespoons Marsala or brandy

1 litre (1 ³/₄ pints) water

sea salt and freshly milled black pepper

1 litre (1 ³/₄ pints) fish stock, kept simmering

2 shallots, very finely chopped

500 g (1 lb 2 oz) risotto rice, preferably Carnaroli

a few drops of Tabasco sauce

5 tablespoons double cream

Method

First of all you need to set about creating the perfect stock. Carefully remove all the white and dark meat from the halved lobsters, reserving any roe. Separate the types of meat and put it to one side. Make sure you discard the intestinal vein, gills, liver and stomach. Now take the carcasses and pound them into a coarse purée. Put this mixture into a deep pan with half the butter, the celery, carrot, onion and herbs. Fry all this together until the vegetables are soft, then pour over the Marsala or brandy. Light the alcohol by tipping the pan over a gas flame or lighting with a taper, and burn off the alcohol, then pour in the water. Season with salt and pepper and simmer this stock for about 1 hour, uncovered, stirring occasionally. Cool and strain carefully. You should end up with about 500 ml (17 fl oz) of very intensely flavoured stock.

Now heat both the stocks in separate pans and keep them at a simmer. In a third pan, fry the shallots gently in the remaining butter until soft. Add all the rice and fry together until the grains are shiny and crackling hot. Add a ladleful of the hot lobster stock and wait for it to be absorbed as you gently stir, then add fish stock in the same way, then lobster stock. Continue in this way, alternating the two stocks for about 10 minutes until the rice is half cooked. Then add all the lobster meat and any roe, stir thoroughly and resume the cooking process.

When the risotto is creamy, tender and velvety but the grains are still firm in the centre, take it off the heat and stir in the Tabasco sauce and the cream. Adjust the seasoning, stir and cover. Leave the risotto to rest for about 3 minutes, then turn on to a warmed platter and serve at once.

Seafood Risotto
Risotto ai Frutti di Mare

I'll give you a basic outline of the right quantities to use for this symphony of flavours, but you must not be at all restricted. Feel free to use whatever seafood you think is appropriate and looks delicious at the time.

SERVES 4–6

450 g (I lb) baby clams, scrubbed and
    thoroughly cleaned

I bottle dry white wine

450 g (I lb) fresh, live mussels, scrubbed
    and thoroughly cleaned

150 ml (5 fl oz) extra virgin olive oil

225 g (8 oz) white fish fillet

sea salt and freshly milled black pepper

225 g (8 oz) raw, shell-on small prawns

225 g (8 oz) raw, shell-on langoustines
    or large prawns

1.2 litres (2 pints) strong fish stock,
    kept simmering

I cooked crab, split open

1/2 dried red chilli pepper, finely chopped

3 garlic cloves, finely chopped

3 tablespoons chopped fresh parsley

500 g (I lb 2 oz) risotto rice, preferably
    Carnaroli

Method

All the raw seafood will need to be cooked separately in the first instance. Wash and clean everything really carefully. Place the baby clams in a large pan with a glass of wine and shake over a medium heat for about 6 minutes until open. Discard any which remain closed. Remove three-quarters of the clams from their shells and set them aside with the remainder still in their shells. Strain the juices from the pan through a fine sieve into a bowl. Next, do exactly the same with the mussels.

Heat 2 tablespoons of oil in a frying pan and fry the fish fillet on both sides for about 5 minutes until tender, basting with a little of the wine to keep the fish very soft. Season with salt and pepper and flake it roughly, discarding any skin. Put it to one side until required.

Heat 3 tablespoons of oil in another pan and quickly fry the prawns until bright pink and cooked through, turning frequently and basting with a little wine. Peel the prawns and set them aside. Add the shells and heads to the simmering fish stock.

Heat a further 3 tablespoons of oil and quickly fry the langoustines or large prawns until pink and cooked through, turning frequently and basting with a little wine. Remove from the pan and take off the legs and claws. Open them out and remove all the flesh from inside. Put the claws, legs and reserved flesh with the peeled prawns for later use and add the carcasses to the stock. Discard anything inedible, such as the intestinal tube. (If you are using giant prawns, simply shell half and leave the other half with their shells on. Put the shells with the fish stock.)

Remove all the dark and white meat from the crab's body, taking care to leave all the intestines behind. Reserve the claws. Do not add the crab shell, the intestines or any other debris from the crab to the stock.

Strain the stock and return it to a simmer.

Now use all the remaining oil to fry the chilli, garlic and parsley together for 2 minutes, then add the rice and stir thoroughly to coat the rice all over and make it crackling hot. Add a glass of wine, stir and boil for 2 minutes to evaporate the alcohol. Add the juices from the clams and mussels, stir and allow the grains to absorb this liquid, then begin to alternate additions of wine and hot stock. When the wine has been used, continue with only stock. Carry on in this way for about 12 minutes until the risotto is about two-thirds cooked, then add all the cooked seafood and fish including the shells, legs and claws. Stir together thoroughly and continue to cook as before, adding fish stock gradually and stirring. When the rice is creamy but still firm in the centre, transfer to a warmed platter, arranging the claws and shells on the top. Serve at once.

Fiammetta's Risotto
Il Risotto di Fiammetta

This is possibly my favourite of all the elaborate risotti and is one which my mother Fiammetta has made so many times over the years that it has become a firm family standby recipe. The end result needs to be quite fluid.

SERVES 6

2 kg (4¹/₂ lb) fresh, live mussels, scrubbed and thoroughly cleaned

I kg (2¹/₄ lb) baby clams, scrubbed and thoroughly cleaned

I onion, chopped

2 leeks, whites only, chopped

50 g (2 oz) unsalted butter

4 tablespoons dry white wine

3 large, sweet, ripe and squashy tomatoes, skinned, seeded and coarsely chopped

500 g (I lb 2 oz) risotto rice

1.5 litres (2¹/₂ pints) hot water

sea salt and freshly milled black pepper

I teaspoon saffron powder

I bay leaf

I bunch of fresh parsley stalks

Method

Place the mussels and clams in a large pan, cover and shake the pan over a medium heat until all the shells have opened. Any shells which have not opened after about 8 minutes are not going to and should be discarded. Take all the molluscs out of their shells and set aside. Strain the liquid carefully through muslin and set that aside also.

Fry the onion and leeks in the butter until soft, then add the wine and boil off the alcohol for a minute or so. Add the tomatoes, the reserved liquid from the mussels and clams, and the rice and stir well. Add all the water to the pan, season with salt and pepper and add the saffron, bay leaf and parsley stalks. Stir and simmer gently for about 20 minutes until the rice is tender and the risotto is creamy. Add the mussels and clams and heat through. Remove the bay leaf and parsley stalks and serve at once on a warmed platter.

Risotto with Squid
Risotto con le Seppie

Cleaning squid is a messy, fiddly business, especially if they are small. A good fishmonger will do it for you. Squid can be served immediately it becomes tender, or after a long stewing process. Make sure the squid is tender before you add the rice.

SERVES 6

400 g (14 oz) fresh or thawed frozen squid

2 onions, finely chopped

2–4 garlic cloves, finely chopped

75 ml (3 fl oz) olive oil

1 large glass of dry white wine

sea salt and freshly milled black pepper

1 teaspoon concentrated tomato purée

300 g (11 oz) risotto rice

2 litres (3½ pints) vegetable or fish stock, kept simmering

a handful of chopped fresh parsley

Method

Clean the squid carefully, removing the beak, the eye and the skin. Cut the cleaned squid into small pieces, wash and dry carefully.

Fry the onions and garlic together in the oil until the onions are softened but not coloured. Add the squid and cook gently for about 10 minutes, sprinkling with the wine as you stir. As soon as the squid is tender, season with salt and pepper, add the tomato purée and stir carefully, then add all the rice. Don't be tempted to add the rice until the squid is tender. Add a ladleful of hot stock at a time, allowing the rice to absorb the liquid after each addition and before the next one. Continue in this way for about 20 minutes until the rice is tender. Then take the pan off the heat, cover and leave the risotto to rest for about 3 minutes. Transfer to a warmed dish, sprinkle with parsley and serve at once.

Risotto with Cuttlefish Ink
Risotto Nero alle Seppie

You can buy cuttlefish with their ink sacs at fishmongers but you can also buy them separately. Squid are sold without ink and the ink is sold in small, sanitized sachets ready to use.

SERVES 4–6

750 g (1¾ lb) cuttlefish with ink sacs

1.2 litres (2 pints) fish stock,
   kept simmering

½ onion, finely chopped

1 garlic clove, finely chopped

3 tablespoons extra virgin olive oil

500 g (1 lb 2 oz) risotto rice, preferably
   Vialone Nano

120 ml (4 fl oz) dry white wine

1 tablespoon unsalted butter

3 tablespoons finely chopped fresh
   flatleaf parsley

sea salt and freshly milled black pepper

Method

Rinse the cuttlefish, remove the tentacles and head. Carefully remove the ink sacs from the heads without splitting them. Discard the yellow sac in this instance. Put the ink sacs into a strainer over a small bowl, and use the back of a teaspoon to press out the ink. Pour a few tablespoons of the fish stock over the sacs and leave to drain and thus extract the rest of the ink. Prepare the cuttlefish by removing all the internal organs and the back bone. Wash thoroughly and cut the flesh into thin rings and strips.

Fry the onion and garlic in the oil until translucent and soft but not brown. Add the cuttlefish and cook gently for about 20 minutes until tender, adding a little stock to the pan if necessary during cooking. Add all the rice in one go and stir together thoroughly. When the grains are lightly toasted, add the wine and the ink and stir together until hot. Begin to add the hot stock, one ladleful at a time. Keep stirring and remember always to allow the liquid to be absorbed before adding any more. Remember also to scrape down the sides carefully. As soon as the risotto is cooked, 18–20 minutes later, take it off the heat and stir in the butter, parsley and salt and pepper to taste. Cover and leave to rest for 2–3 minutes, then stir again and turn out on to warmed plates or a warmed serving platter to serve.

5 *Meat*

When making a risotto with meat, the question of which stock to use becomes even more all-important than for other risotti. For example, would you choose a vegetable stock or a lamb stock when making Lamb Risotto with Courgettes? And just how potent should the game stock be when making the Wild Boar Risotto? These questions, and no doubt countless others, are very hard for me to help you with unless I am in the kitchen with you while you are cooking!

As I have said so often in the past, what distinguishes a good cook from an excellent cook has actually nothing to do with technique, which can be taught, but everything to do with instinct, which cannot be taught. Common sense and experience are also helpful! So taste the stock and think about how it will carry or smother the flavour of the meat, then make your decision. Remember you can always change the flavour of the stock either by diluting it with more water or intensifying it by fierce boiling to a reduction. Once it is mixed with the rice, however, it will be too late for either of these options.

The great classics in this chapter, not to be missed, are the Classic Milanese Saffron Risotto (page 121), the Chicken Liver Risotto (page 137), the Risotto of the Guards of the Serene Republic (page 124) and both the ragu risotti (pages 117 and 118). I know a lot of people will feel squeamish about the Veal Sweetbread Risotto on page 136, but I had to include it just because it tastes so fantastically delicious.

Risotto with a White Ragu
Risotto al Ragu Bianco

Any white meat will work for this recipe so chicken, turkey, rabbit or veal are all fine. It also works with lamb, but the result is very different. For a proper lamb risotto see page 120. The 'white' in the recipe title actually refers to the fact that no tomato is used.

SERVES 4

1 onion, chopped

1 celery stick, chopped

75 g (3 oz) unsalted butter

400 g (14 oz) boned chicken, turkey
   or rabbit, cubed

finely grated zest and juice of ¹/₂ lemon

1 glass dry white wine

sea salt and freshly milled black pepper

1.2 litres (2 pints) chicken stock,
   kept simmering

400 g (14 oz) risotto rice

5 tablespoons single cream

50 g (2 oz) Parmesan cheese,
   freshly grated

2 teaspoons chopped fresh parsley

Method

Fry the onion and celery together gently in half the butter until the vegetables are soft. Add the meat and fry until browned all over, then add the lemon zest and juice and stir together. Add the wine, season and simmer together for about 15 minutes, basting with a little of the hot stock if necessary, until the meat is tender. Add the rice and stir together thoroughly, then begin to add the hot stock, stirring constantly and allowing the liquid to be absorbed before adding more. Continue to cook the rice in this way, making sure that the rice always absorbs the stock before you add more liquid. Check the seasoning about half way through. After about 20 minutes, when the risotto is creamy and velvety but the rice grains are still firm to the bite, take it off the heat and stir in the remaining butter, the cream and the Parmesan. Stir and cover. Leave to rest for about 2–3 minutes, then transfer to a warmed platter, sprinkle with the parsley and serve at once.

Risotto with Tomato Ragu
Risotto al Ragu con Pomodoro

You need to begin with a rich ragu sauce for this risotto to really be outstanding. Allow yourself plenty time and make the ragu the day before so that the flavours have time to develop.

SERVES 6

1 carrot, chopped

1 celery stick, chopped

1 onion, chopped

4 tablespoons extra virgin olive oil

1 slice prosciutto crudo, chopped

250 g (9 oz) minced beef or veal

1 glass dry red wine

400 g (14 oz) thick passata

1/2 bay leaf

sea salt and freshly milled black pepper

500 g (1 lb 2 oz) risotto rice

1.5 litres (2 1/2 pints) chicken or beef stock, kept simmering

25 g (1 oz) unsalted butter

50 g (2 oz) Parmesan cheese, freshly grated

Method

Make the ragu first, preferably the day before. Fry together all the vegetables with the oil and the prosciutto until the vegetables are soft. Add the minced meat and the wine and fry until the meat is brown and the alcohol has boiled away. Then add the passata and the bay leaf and season with salt and pepper. Cover and leave to simmer gently for about 2 hours or until rich and dense with a bright orange rim.

If you have made this ahead of time, take it off the heat, cool, chill and refrigerate until required. If not, carry on from this point by adding the rice to the ragu. Stir until the rice is looking very dry, then begin to add the hot stock, a ladleful at a time, stirring constantly and allowing the liquid to be absorbed before adding more. Continue to cook the rice in this way for about 20 minutes, making sure that the rice always absorbs the stock before you add more liquid. When the risotto is creamy and velvety but the rice grains are still firm to the bite, take it off the heat. Discard the bay leaf and stir in the butter and Parmesan. Adjust the seasoning. Cover and leave to rest for about 3 minutes, then transfer to a warmed platter and serve at once.

Lamb Risotto with Courgettes
Risotto d'Agnello con Zucchine

A rich and sweet-tasting risotto, this is very filling, so like many of the meat risotti it makes a good main course with perhaps just a fresh and crisp green salad to follow.

SERVES 4

1 onion, chopped

1 celery stick, chopped

2 courgettes, diced

75 g (3 oz) unsalted butter

250 g (9 oz) lamb steaks, trimmed
  and cubed

1 glass dry white wine

400 g (14 oz) Arborio rice

1.2 litres (2 pints) chicken or
  vegetable stock, kept simmering

sea salt and freshly milled black pepper

2 tablespoons finely chopped fresh mint

3 tablespoons freshly grated Pecorino

Method

Fry the onion, celery and courgettes together in half the butter until soft. Add the lamb and brown carefully all over, then add the wine and simmer for 1 minute to burn off the alcohol. Add the rice and mix together thoroughly, then begin to add the hot stock gradually. Always add the stock one ladleful at a time and stir in between each addition. Do not add more stock until the previous quantity has been absorbed. As you continue to cook the rice in this way, it will slowly turn creamy and velvety. When the risotto reaches this stage but the grains are still firm in the centre, the risotto is cooked and ready to be finished off. Take it off the heat, stir in the rest of the butter, the mint and the Pecorino. Stir, adjust the seasoning and cover. Leave it to rest for a couple of minutes, then transfer it to a warmed platter and serve at once.

Classic Milanese Saffron Risotto
Risotto alla Milanese Classico

The traditional recipe for this much-loved risotto includes beef bone marrow, which in recent times has been an extremely contentious ingredient. It is very much my hope that we can all go back to enjoying beef and all its offal and extras without any worries. If you are concerned, consider a switch to organic beef bone marrow for this recipe. For a simpler (and bone marrow free) version of this recipe, see page 88. The stock for this risotto is traditionally made with veal, beef and chicken and assorted vegetables but absolutely no tomato.

SERVES 6

½ onion, finely chopped

100 g (4 oz) unsalted butter

40 g (1½ oz) raw beef bone
    marrow, chopped

500 g (1 lb 2 oz) risotto rice,
    preferably Vialone Gigante

1.5 litres (2½ pints) rich stock,
    kept simmering

1 sachet of saffron powder

50 g (2 oz) Parmesan cheese,
    freshly grated, plus extra for serving

sea salt and freshly milled black pepper

Method

Soak the onion in cold water for about 10 minutes, then drain and squeeze dry in a napkin. Fry the onion very gently in half the butter with the beef marrow until the onion is soft, then add the rice. Stir to coat the grains thoroughly until the rice grains are crackling hot but not coloured. Begin to add the hot stock, stirring constantly and allowing the liquid to be absorbed before adding more. Continue to cook the rice in this way, making sure that the rice always absorbs the stock before you add more liquid. Half way through cooking, after about 10 minutes, add the saffron powder and stir through thoroughly. When the risotto is creamy and velvety but the rice grains are still firm to the bite, take it off the heat. Stir in the rest of the butter and the Parmesan and season with salt and pepper. Cover and leave to rest for a couple of minutes, then stir again and transfer to a warmed platter. Serve at once, offering extra grated Parmesan at the table.

Sardinian Saffron Risotto
Risotto Sardo allo Zafferano

An unusual risotto, this one is from Sardinia, where small quantities of rice are grown, thus making rice a tiny part of the local traditional menu. Saffron also grows on this most beautiful island, though disappointingly it seldom appears in the island's repertoire of recipes. This is the only region of Italy where saffron is used in strands instead of powder. This risotto is sometimes served with *Ossobucco*.

SERVES 6

75 g (3 oz) pork dripping, lard
   or pork belly

1 large onion, finely chopped

300 g (11 oz) hand or shoulder
   of pork, finely cubed

1/2 glass dry white wine

300 g (11 oz) fresh, juicy, ripe tomatoes,
   skinned and roughly chopped

a pinch of saffron strands, soaked
   in a little warm water

500 g (1 lb 2 oz) risotto rice

1.5 litres (2 1/2 pints) pork stock,
   kept simmering

50 g (2 oz) freshly grated
   Pecorino cheese

sea salt and freshly milled
   black pepper

Method

Fry the pork dripping with the onion until the onion is soft, then add the pork cubes. Cook together, basting with the wine, until the pork is browned all over. Add the tomatoes and mix together thoroughly, then pour in the saffron and the water in which it was soaking. Continue to simmer gently, adding a little stock as necessary, for about 1 hour until the pork is falling into shreds.

Add the rice and stir until all the grains are coated and very hot. Begin to add the hot stock, stirring constantly and allowing the liquid to be absorbed before adding more. Continue to cook the rice in this way, making sure that the rice always absorbs the stock before you add more liquid. When the risotto is creamy and velvety but the rice grains are still firm to the bite, take it off the heat. Stir in the Pecorino, season with salt and pepper and cover. Rest the risotto for 2–3 minutes, then stir again, transfer to a warmed platter, grind a little extra pepper over the top and serve at once.

The Risotto of the Guards of the Serene Republic

Risotto alla Sbirraglia

This is also known as *Sbirri!* It is a typically Venetian risotto, very wet and runny, but also very rich and filling.

SERVES 4

½ onion, finely chopped

100 g (4 oz) unsalted butter

500 g (1 lb 2 oz) skinless
   chicken fillet, cubed

1 glass dry white wine

400 g (14 oz) risotto rice, preferably
   Vialone Gigante

1.2 litres (2 pints) rich chicken stock,
   kept simmering

75 g (3 oz) Parmesan cheese, freshly grated

sea salt and freshly milled black pepper

Method

Fry the onion in half the butter until just pale golden, then add the chicken cubes. Cook the chicken really gently until lightly browned, then pour in the wine and cook quickly for about 2 minutes to allow the alcohol to burn off. Add the rice and stir thoroughly until hot and shining. Lower the heat, then add the hot stock gradually, one ladleful at a time, stirring continuously until the liquid is absorbed. Continue in this way for about 20 minutes until all the stock has been used and the rice is tender. Stir in the remaining butter and half the Parmesan and season with salt and pepper. Remove from the heat and cover. Leave to rest for about 3 minutes, transfer to a warmed platter, sprinkle with the remaining Parmesan and serve.

Frogs' Legs Risotto
Risotto alle Rane

It is always best to buy your frogs' legs ready cleaned because cleaning them is extremely tricky and very time consuming. I know of two versions of this very popular risotto, one from Milan and the other from Piedmont. What follows is a blend of the two versions.

SERVES 6

1 kg (2¼ lb) frogs' legs, cleaned
  and skinned

2 onions

1 celery stick, quartered

sea salt and freshly milled black pepper

100 g (4 oz) unsalted butter

2 garlic cloves, chopped

120 ml (4 fl oz) beef stock, kept simmering

a large handful of fresh flatleaf parsley,
  chopped

500 g (1 lb 2 oz) risotto rice

Method

Bring a pot of salted water to the boil and plunge in the frogs' legs. Boil for 5–6 minutes until the meat comes away from the bones easily. Scoop the frogs' legs out of the water with a slotted spoon. Remove all the meat and set aside. Return the carcasses to the water; this will become your stock. Quarter 1 onion and add half to the stock with the celery. Season, bring to the boil, then simmer for about 30 minutes. Strain into a clean pan, then return to a simmer.

Meanwhile, fry the remaining onion quarters in half the butter with the garlic and the meat from the frogs' legs. When the onion is cooked, baste with a little of the meat stock to moisten the mixture and season with salt and pepper. Simmer gently until well blended and moist, then add 2 tablespoons of chopped parsley and keep warm.

Chop the remaining onion and begin to make the risotto. Fry the onion in the remaining butter until soft, then add the rice and toast the grains. Begin to add the strained frog stock, making sure the rice absorbs all the liquid before adding any more. Keep stirring and adding stock gradually for about 20 minutes until the risotto is creamy but the rice still firm to the bite. Season to taste and stir in all the remaining parsley. Transfer to a warmed platter, pour the frog mixture on top and serve immediately.

Duck Risotto
Risotto all'Anatra

I prefer to use wild duck for this sort of recipe as it tends to be less fatty. I would also strongly recommend that you ask the butcher or game dealer to bone the duck for you and get him to give you all the carcass and skin to make your stock. Alternatively, use six to eight skinned duck breasts.

SERVES 6

1 wild or domestic duck weighing about 2 kg (2¼ lb), plucked, gutted and boned (use the carcass to make a rich duck stock see page 29)

2 onions, finely chopped

2 garlic cloves, lightly crushed

75 ml (3 fl oz) extra virgin olive oil

4 fresh sage leaves, chopped

½ bottle dry white wine

1 tablespoon concentrated tomato purée

75 g (3 oz) unsalted butter

sea salt and freshly milled black pepper

500 g (1 lb 2 oz) risotto rice, preferably Carnaroli

1.5 litres (2½ pints) duck stock, kept simmering

3 tablespoons freshly grated Parmesan cheese

Method

Trim all the duck meat and cut it into neat cubes. Fry the onions and garlic with the olive oil until soft and translucent. Add the sage and the duck. Brown the duck meat all over thoroughly, then add the wine and stir. Raise the heat and burn off the alcohol for about 1 minute, then add the tomato purée, half the butter and the seasoning. Cover and simmer for about 40 minutes until the duck is tender, occasionally adding a little wine or water if it appears to be sticking. When the duck is cooked, add all the rice in one go and stir thoroughly. Then begin to add the hot stock, stirring constantly and allowing the liquid to be absorbed before adding more. Continue to cook the rice in this way, making sure that the rice always absorbs the stock before you add more liquid. This will take about 20 minutes. When the risotto is creamy and velvety but the rice grains are still firm to the bite, take it off the heat. Stir in the rest of the butter and the Parmesan, adjust the seasoning and then cover. Leave to stand for 2 minutes, then transfer to a warmed platter and serve at once.

Wild Boar Risotto
Risotto al Cinghiale

I love the taste of wild boar, although I know some people find it rather too strong and gamey. Farmed boar is not as strong as the boar I am used to hunting and eating in Tuscany, but it is definitely stronger than pork. It really does marry very well with the porcini mushrooms and the red wine. Don't underestimate how tough this meat can be if not well treated, however, especially if it is wild. Remember that the longer you leave the meat to marinate, the more tender and delicious it will become.

SERVES 6

500 g (1 lb 2 oz) boar stewing steak

½ bottle very full-bodied red wine
such as Barolo

1 sprig of fresh rosemary

a handful of crushed black
peppercorns

1 cinnamon stick, broken

1 celery stick, chopped

1 onion, chopped

1 garlic clove, chopped

1 large carrot, chopped

6 tablespoons very fruity extra
virgin olive oil

a small handful of dried porcini mushrooms,
soaked in a bowl of warm water for about
20 minutes or overnight

3 tablespoons concentrated tomato purée

sea salt and freshly milled black pepper

500 g (1 lb 2 oz) Arborio rice

1.2 litres (2 pints) game or chicken stock,
kept simmering

3 tablespoons freshly grated
Parmesan cheese

Method

Trim the meat and cut it all into small cubes, no bigger than a walnut. Mix together the wine, rosemary, peppercorns and cinnamon in a glass or ceramic dish. Put the meat into the marinade and leave it there for a couple of hours or up to a day. Take the meat out and strain the marinade, reserving both.

Now fry together the celery, onion, garlic and carrot with the olive oil until the vegetables are all soft. Drain the mushrooms, straining and reserving the liquid, then chop them coarsely. Stir them into the vegetables, baste with carefully strained liquid from the mushrooms, then add the boar and stir. Add the strained marinade and the tomato purée, stir and simmer, covered, for about 2 hours or until the meat is very tender.

Adjust the seasoning, then add the rice and stir together thoroughly until the rice has absorbed all the available liquid. Then begin to add the hot stock, a ladleful at a time, stirring constantly and allowing the liquid to be absorbed before adding more. Continue to cook the rice in this way for about 20 minutes, making sure that the rice always absorbs the stock before you add more liquid. When the risotto is creamy and velvety but the rice grains are still firm to the bite, take it off the heat. Stir in the Parmesan, adjust the seasoning and cover. Leave the rice to rest for about 3 minutes, then transfer to a warmed platter and serve at once.

VARIATIONS

Should you really find the flavour and texture of boar is not to your liking, you might consider using organic, outdoor-reared pork, which has a much milder flavour but which also complements the flavours of the porcini and wine. As another alternative, you could use the same weight of pigeon breasts, wild duck breasts or guinea fowl, all of which will give you plenty of gamey flavour, although will not be quite as strong as the boar. If you want to change the flavour of the marinade and therefore of the risotto, you can also use half wine and half balsamic vinegar.

Rabbit Risotto with Olives
Risotto al Coniglio con le Olive

I think rabbit provides us with a delicious and much underestimated meat source. It is such a shame that so many people allow their sentimental feelings to mean they will never try this cheap and readily available delicacy. In my area of Tuscany, where this way of cooking rabbit originates, they grow a special olive just for this purpose. In the absence of *olive per il coniglio* you need to find some small, sweet, slightly wrinkly olives with a bittersweet flavour. Do not be tempted to use the rabbit carcass for the stock as you will get a result which is far too sickly sweet.

SERVES 4

1 rabbit, boned

1 onion, chopped

1 celery stick, chopped

a handful of fresh flatleaf parsley, chopped

4 tablespoons extra virgin olive oil

4 slices pancetta or prosciutto crudo, chopped

2 tablespoons concentrated tomato purée

1 glass dry red wine

about 18–20 stoned black olives, coarsely chopped

a pinch of dried oregano

sea salt and freshly milled black pepper

400 g (14 oz) risotto rice

1.2 litres (2 pints) chicken or vegetable stock, kept simmering

Method

Wash and dry all the rabbit meat, then set it aside until required. Make sure none of the pieces is larger than a walnut. Fry the onion, celery and parsley with the oil and pancetta or prosciutto until the onion is soft. Add the rabbit and brown the rabbit all over. Mix together the tomato purée and wine and stir into the rabbit mixture. Add the olives and oregano, season and stir, then cover and simmer for about 1½ hours or until the rabbit is really tender and flaking. Make sure that this mixture remains very moist by occasionally adding a little stock or some wine.

When the rabbit is cooked, pour in the rice and stir to coat all the grains. Then begin to add the hot stock, a ladleful at a time, stirring constantly and allowing the liquid to be absorbed before adding more. Continue to cook the rice in this way for about 20 minutes, making sure that the rice always absorbs the stock before you add more liquid. When the risotto is creamy and velvety but the rice grains are still firm to the bite, take it off the heat. Adjust the seasoning, then transfer to a warmed platter and serve at once.

Hare Risotto
Risotto alla Lepre

It is always a good idea to let the hare marinate for a day or so before use as this will make it much more tender and will reduce the cooking time considerably.

SERVES 4

FOR THE MARINADE:

1/2 bottle full-bodied red wine

1 teaspoon balsamic vinegar

2 tablespoons extra virgin olive oil

3 juniper berries, lightly crushed

4 black peppercorns, lightly crushed

1 bay leaf, bruised

FOR THE RISOTTO:

300 g (11 oz) hare meat, boned and cubed

75 g (3 oz) very fatty prosciutto crudo

1 onion, finely chopped

1 celery stick, chopped

1 carrot, chopped

3 fresh sage leaves, chopped

1 garlic clove, chopped

1 tablespoon concentrated tomato purée

5 tablespoons Marsala

400 g (14 oz) Arborio rice

1.2 litres (2 pints) game stock,
   kept simmering

1 tablespoon unsalted butter

2–3 tablespoons freshly grated
   Parmesan cheese

sea salt and freshly milled black pepper

Method

First of all mix the marinade ingredients together and lay the hare in the liquid to soak for about a day, or certainly overnight. Remove the meat from the marinade. Strain and reserve the marinade for later use.

Fry the prosciutto with the onion, celery, carrot, sage and garlic until all the vegetables are soft, then add the tomato purée, Marsala and hare. Mix together thoroughly, basting occasionally with the marinade for 1–1 1/2 hours until the hare is completely cooked and beginning to fall to bits.

Add the rice and stir together until the rice is well coated and reasonably dry, having absorbed most of the available liquid. Then begin to add the hot stock, a ladleful at a time, stirring constantly and allowing the liquid to be absorbed before adding more. Continue to cook the rice in this way for about 20 minutes, making sure that the rice always absorbs the stock before you add more liquid. When the risotto is creamy and velvety but the rice grains are still firm to the bite, take it off the heat. Stir in the butter and Parmesan and adjust the seasoning. Cover and leave to rest for about 3 minutes, then stir again and transfer to a warmed dish to serve.

Italian Sausage Risotto
Risotto alla Luganega

If you cannot find *Luganega* sausage, which is easy to recognise because it is made in a continuous coil, then opt for the same weight of other Italian sausages. Do not confuse a raw Italian *salsiccia* with a cured sausage like salami.

SERVES 6

75 g (3 oz) unsalted butter

I large onion, finely chopped

450 g (I lb) *Luganega* or other raw Italian
  sausage, peeled and crumbled

a handful of dried porcini mushrooms, soaked
  in a bowl of warm water for 20 minutes

I tablespoon concentrated tomato purée

1.5 litres (2½ pints) beef or chicken stock,
  kept simmering

500 g (I lb 2 oz) Arborio rice

sea salt and freshly milled black pepper

50 g (2 oz) Parmesan cheese, freshly
  grated, plus extra for serving

Method

Heat half the butter and fry the onion gently with the sausage until the onion is soft and the sausage cooked through. Drain the mushrooms and reserve the liquid. Chop the mushrooms coarsely and add to the pot. Stir and cook for a few minutes, basting with the strained liquid from the mushrooms. Add the tomato purée and stir together. Cover and simmer for about 15 minutes, stirring and adding a little stock from time to time if necessary. Add the rice all in one go and stir thoroughly. When the rice has heated through, add the first ladleful of hot stock and stir again. Continue adding stock and stirring, making sure the rice absorbs all the liquid each time before adding any more. This will take about 20 minutes. Season to taste with salt and pepper. When the rice is creamy and velvety but the grains are still firm to the bite, take the risotto off the heat. Stir in the rest of the butter and the Parmesan, cover and leave to rest for 2 minutes, then stir again and transfer to a warmed platter to serve at once. Serve extra Parmesan separately at the table.

Parma Ham Risotto
Risotto al Prosciutto di Parma

Although rice dishes are not traditional of the Parma area, we can make an exception with this particular recipe in which the rich flavour of the ham combines extremely well with the rice, the white wine and the stock to make a fantastically creamy risotto which will soon become a favourite.

SERVES 4–6

1 smallish onion, very finely chopped

50 g (2 oz) unsalted butter

250 g (9 oz) Parma ham, thinly sliced
  and cut into strips

400 g (14 oz) risotto rice, preferably
  Arborio or Carnaroli

1 large glass dry white wine

1.5 litres (2½ pints) chicken, pork and
  vegetable stock, kept simmering

1 tablespoon unsalted butter

75 g (3 oz) Parmesan cheese, freshly grated

salt if necessary

freshly milled black pepper

Method

Fry the onion gently in the butter without letting it colour. Add half the ham and fry for a few minutes, then add all the rice in one go. Toast the rice grains carefully all over, turning the rice frequently in the fat. When the rice is well toasted and shiny, add the wine and stir quickly for 2 minutes to evaporate the alcohol, then add the first ladleful of hot stock. Continue to stir constantly, only adding more stock when the previous quantity of liquid has been absorbed, for about 20 minutes. When the rice is tender and all the grains are evenly swollen but still firm in the centre, take the risotto off the heat and stir in the remaining ham, the butter and half the Parmesan. Stir vigorously and adjust the seasoning as necessary. Cover and leave to rest for 3 minutes, then transfer to a warm platter and sprinkle with the rest of the Parmesan. Serve at once.

Risotto with Pancetta and Leeks
Risotto con Pancetta e Porri

The taste of pancetta is very distinctive and quite different from bacon. Fortunately it is very widely available these days, so you really should not have any trouble finding it. If you are unlucky and cannot find it, the only possible substitute for this recipe is really top quality, green streaky bacon.

SERVES 4

3 tablespoons extra virgin olive oil

400 g (14 oz) leeks, finely chopped

150 g (5 oz) thinly sliced pancetta, chopped

400 g (14 oz) Arborio rice

1 litre (1³/₄ pints) chicken or vegetable stock, kept simmering

50 g (2 oz) unsalted butter

50 g (2 oz) Parmesan cheese, freshly grated

sea salt and freshly milled black pepper

Method

Fry the oil, leeks and pancetta together thoroughly until the leeks are cooked through and soft. Add the rice and stir thoroughly to coat all the grains. Then begin to add the hot stock, stirring constantly and allowing the liquid to be absorbed before adding more. Continue to cook the rice in this way for about 20 minutes, making sure that the rice always absorbs the stock before you add more liquid. When the risotto is creamy and velvety but the rice grains are still firm to the bite, take it off the heat. Stir in the butter and Parmesan and adjust the seasoning. Cover and leave to rest for about 3 minutes. Stir again and transfer to a warmed platter and serve at once.

Veal Sweetbread Risotto
Risotto alle Animelle

Y ou can also make the same dish using lamb sweetbreads or a combination (half and half) of lamb sweetbreads and lambs' liver. I know a lot of people feel very squeamish about sweetbreads, but if you can overcome your prejudice enough to just taste them, they are indescribably delicious.

SERVES 6

1 onion, finely chopped

100 g (4 oz) unsalted butter

75 g (3 oz) slices prosciutto crudo,
   cut into strips

175 g (6 oz) sweetbreads, cleaned
   and trimmed

1 glass dry white wine

sea salt and freshly milled black pepper

500 g (1 lb 2 oz) Arborio rice

1.5 litres (2½ pints) veal or lamb stock,
   kept simmering

50 g (2 oz) Parmesan cheese,
   freshly grated

Method

Fry the onion gently in half the butter until soft and translucent. Add the prosciutto and sweetbreads, mix together and simmer gently for a few minutes. Gradually add the wine, season with salt and pepper and cook gently for about 10–12 minutes, depending on size, until the sweetbreads are cooked through and you have a thick, rich texture. Add the rice and coat carefully with this base, stirring constantly until the rice is very hot. Then begin to add the hot stock, stirring constantly and allowing the liquid to be absorbed before adding more. Continue to cook the rice in this way for about 20 minutes, making sure that the rice always absorbs the stock before you add more liquid. When the risotto is creamy and velvety but the rice grains are still firm to the bite, take it off the heat. Add the remaining butter and the Parmesan and adjust the seasoning. Stir and cover. Leave to rest for 2–3 minutes, then stir again and transfer to a warmed platter. Serve at once.

Chicken Liver Risotto
Risotto di Fegatini

When buying and using chicken livers, please make sure you don't ruin the whole dish by using chicken livers that are not properly cleaned. As an alternative to chicken livers you could use trimmed and cleaned calves' liver sliced into very small pieces.

SERVES 6

175 g (6 oz) chicken livers

75 g (3 oz) unsalted butter

I onion, finely chopped

I small carrot, finely chopped

I small celery stick, finely chopped

500 g (I lb 2 oz) risotto rice, preferably Carnaroli

I large glass dry white wine

1.5 litres (2½ pints) chicken stock, kept simmering

sea salt and freshly milled black pepper

75 g (3 oz) Parmesan cheese, freshly grated

Method

Carefully pick over and clean the chicken livers, removing any trace of bile. Wash them thoroughly, then dry, trim carefully and chop coarsely. Fry half the butter gently with the onion, carrot and celery until all the vegetables are soft, then add the chicken livers and fry gently together for a few more minutes until the livers are well browned. Add the rice and mix together until the rice is crackling hot. Pour over the wine and wait for the alcohol to evaporate, then begin gradually to add the hot stock, stirring after each addition and making sure the rice has absorbed the liquid before adding any more. Season with salt and pepper and carry on the cooking process for about 20 minutes until you have a smooth velvety texture, but making sure the grains are still firm to the bite in the centre. Take the risotto off the heat and stir in the remaining butter and the Parmesan. Cover and rest the risotto for 3 minutes, then stir and transfer to a warmed platter to serve at once.

6

Fruit, Alcohol and Sweet

I know just how crazy the idea of putting fruit into a risotto and then serving it as a first course must sound if you have never tried it. However, if you have ever tasted a strawberry, apple, orange or lemon risotto, you'll know what I am talking about! The trend began a few years ago in Milan, and from its beginning as a fashionable idea, some of the more successful combinations have become established as credible recipes. *Provare per credere*! (Try in order to believe!)

The proverb 'Rice, which is born in water must die in wine' tells us that the combination of rice and wine or other alcoholic drinks works extremely well, provided the stock used is in harmony with the other flavours and that the bulk of the alcohol, which can be unpleasantly acidic in drinks such as wine, is allowed to burn away and not affect the dish. Cooking with alcoholic drinks is actually not all that easy, as you can overboil or underboil and spoil a perfectly good dish. Be judicious!

Sweet risotto is not something I am mad about, but a few desserts using risotto rice do work rather well and I have included these. Maxine's Risotto Ice-cream (page 156) is a slightly loopy idea on paper, but it does actually taste very good indeed, and I have seen *Gelato di Riso* on sale in my favourite Italian ice-cream shop at home. Thank you again, Maxine, for letting me use your recipe. The Sweet Risotto Cake (page 152) is something I have been brought up with since the age of two. Our household, just like all Italian households of the time, was convinced that eggs were a vital form of nourishment – and this cake sure packs in a lot of eggs! Do not be alarmed if the Sweet Chocolate Rice (page 155) seems a bit runny; this is as it should be. Do use the best possible chocolate for really good results.

Apple Risotto
Risotto alle Mele

A most unusual risotto flavoured with a little Gorgonzola and with just that final hit of Aquavit to make it really special. If you want to, you can use pears instead of apples, in which case use pear Aquavit to match.

SERVES 6

1 small onion, very finely chopped

75 g (3 oz) unsalted butter

500 g (1 lb 2 oz) risotto rice

1 glass dry white wine

500 g (1 lb 2 oz) apples, peeled, cored and diced

1.5 litres (2½ pints) vegetable or chicken stock, kept simmering

75 g (3 oz) Gorgonzola, diced

sea salt and freshly milled black pepper

4 tablespoons apple Aquavit

Method

Fry the onion gently in half the butter until soft and translucent. Add all the rice and toast the grains all over until shiny and opaque. Add the wine and stir until the liquid has been absorbed and the alcohol has evaporated. Add the apple cubes and stir, then add a little hot stock and stir until the liquid has been absorbed. Now begin to cook the risotto by adding a ladleful of hot stock, then stirring until it has become absorbed, then adding more stock, stirring and waiting, then more stock and so on. The important things are always to wait for the rice to soak up the stock before you add in any more and to stir constantly so that everything is evenly distributed. About half way through the cooking, after 10 minutes or so, add the Gorgonzola and stir it through until it has melted. Now check the seasoning, bearing in mind how very savoury this particular cheese can be, and continue to add stock and cook as before. At the end, when the risotto is creamy and velvety but the rice grains are still firm to the bite in the middle, stir in the Aquavit, then remove the risotto from the heat. Stir in the rest of the butter and cover. Leave to rest for about 2 minutes, stir again and serve on a warmed platter.

Lemon Risotto
Risotto al Limone

I first tasted this risotto in Sorrento, where the lemons grow so big and fat in the shadow of Vesuvius. I have since made it again with lemons grown in other parts of the world, but like so many things in life, the first time will always be the best and most unforgettable. Please be sure you use unwaxed lemons!

SERVES 4

2 shallots or 1 leek (white only),
  very finely chopped
100 g (4 oz) unsalted butter
400 g (14 oz) risotto rice
1 large glass dry white wine
1.2 litres (2 pints) vegetable stock or
  light chicken stock, kept simmering

100 g (4 oz) full fat cheese such as
  Bel Paese or Fontina, cubed
finely grated zest and juice of 1 large
  or 2 small unwaxed lemons
1 tablespoon Limoncello liqueur
sea salt and freshly milled black pepper
freshly grated Parmesan cheese
  for serving

Method

Fry the shallots or leek very slowly in half the butter until soft and translucent. Add all the rice and toast the grains thoroughly all over, making sure they don't brown. Don't let the shallot brown either. Add half the wine and stir until the liquid has been absorbed and the alcohol has evaporated, then add the rest of the wine and repeat. When all the wine has been used up, add the first ladleful of hot stock and the cubed cheese. Stir together and then begin to add rest of the hot stock, stirring constantly and allowing the liquid to be absorbed before adding more. Continue to cook the rice in this way for about 20 minutes, making sure that the rice always absorbs the stock before you add more liquid. When the risotto is creamy and velvety but the rice grains are still firm to the bite, stir in the lemon zest, lemon juice and Limoncello. Allow the alcohol to boil off for 1 minute, then stir in the remaining butter and check the seasoning. Cover and leave to rest for 1 minute, then transfer to a warm dish and serve at once.

Melon and Ham Risotto
Risotto al Prosciutto e Melone

When this was first suggested to me, I was as horrified – as you probably are right now – but once you have opened up your mind to the idea that you really can make risotto in any flavour and with any combination of ingredients, all that is left to do is enjoy it!

SERVES 4

1 medium-sized Galia or Canteloupe
   melon, peeled and cubed

1 glass of tawny Port

1 small onion, finely chopped

150 g (5 oz) sliced prosciutto
   crudo, chopped

100 g (4 oz) unsalted butter

400 g (14 oz) risotto rice

1.2 litres (2 pints) vegetable stock,
   kept simmering

3 tablespoons double cream

sea salt and freshly milled
   black pepper

4 tablespoons freshly grated
   Parmesan cheese

Method

Put the cubed melon into a bowl and pour over the Port. Leave to stand for 30 minutes. Meanwhile fry the onion and the prosciutto in half the butter until soft and translucent. Add the rice and stir it around to coat it thoroughly and get it absolutely sizzling hot. Drain the melon and add the Port to the rice. Stir until the liquid has been absorbed and the alcohol has evaporated. Begin gradually to add the hot stock, making sure the rice has absorbed all the liquid before adding any more to the pot. Stir constantly and watch the rice all the time to make sure it swells evenly and does not either burn or slop around in too much fluid. When the risotto is creamy and velvety but with a firm centre to each grain, add the cream and the melon. Stir to heat through and distribute the melon, then remove from the heat. Adjust the seasoning and stir in the remaining butter. Cover and leave to stand for about 2 minutes, then stir again and transfer to a warmed platter. You can either sprinkle the Parmesan over the risotto at this point or offer it separately at the table.

Strawberry Risotto
Risotto di Fragole

Gloriously pink and creamy, this risotto depends a lot on plenty of freshly milled black pepper. The Victorians enjoyed black pepper with their strawberries, so this is not new, although the idea of including fruit in a risotto is a very modern idea.

SERVES 4

- 1 small onion or 2 shallots, finely chopped
- 50 g (2 oz) unsalted butter
- 500 g (1 lb 2 oz) risotto rice
- 500 g (1 lb 2 oz) strawberries, washed and hulled
- 2 large glasses red wine
- 1.5 litres (2½ pints) chicken stock, kept simmering
- 5 tablespoons double cream
- 6 tablespoons grated Parmesan cheese, plus extra for serving
- sea salt and freshly milled black pepper

Method

Fry the onion or shallots in the butter until soft and transparent. Add the rice and stir to cover it with butter and onion. Slice half the strawberries thinly and stir them into the rice, then add 1 glass of wine. Allow the strawberries to become pulpy and let the wine evaporate. Then add the second glass of wine and stir. When the wine has been absorbed by the rice, begin to add the hot stock. Stir each ladleful of liquid into the rice, let it become absorbed and then add more liquid. Don't rush this process. After about 15 minutes, stir in most of the remaining strawberries and let them become soft and pulpy. Stir in the cream, the Parmesan and a little salt. Add plenty of pepper and finish off the cooking. Arrange on a warmed platter, decorate with the reserved strawberries and serve at once with extra grated Parmesan for everyone to add their own portion.

Pear and Red Wine Risotto
Risotto alle Pere con il Vino Rosso

I love the combination of pears poached until completely soft and dark in a bottle of red wine. So I decided to try making a risotto out of this special taste. The result is slightly unusual, but I believe it is interesting enough to be part of this collection.

SERVES 6

1 onion, chopped very finely

75 g (3 oz) unsalted butter

1 clove

500 g (1 lb 2 oz) risotto rice

2 glasses dry red wine

500 g (1 lb 2 oz) ripe pears, peeled, cored and cubed

1.5 litres (2½ pints) vegetable stock, kept simmering

a large pinch of ground cinnamon

sea salt and freshly milled black pepper

Method

Fry the onion gently in half the butter with the clove. When the onion is soft and melting, remove and discard the clove, add the rice and stir to toast the grains thoroughly. When the rice is sizzling hot, add the wine and boil off the alcohol, then add all the pear cubes and stir. As soon as the rice and pears are well blended and the grains have absorbed all the wine, add the first ladleful of hot stock. Stir and wait for the stock to have soaked into the rice, then add more stock. Keep doing this until the risotto has become creamy and velvety as a whole, even though the individual grains are still firm to the bite in the centre. At this point take the risotto off the heat and stir in the cinnamon and the remaining butter. Add salt and pepper as required, stir and cover. Leave to rest for about 2 minutes, then stir once more, transfer to a warmed platter and serve.

Vodka and Orange Risotto
Risotto alla Vodka con Arancio

Agood late-night party risotto – a bit mad and wild yet still delicious and very soothing to the palate. Avoid flavoured, cheap vodka at all costs!

SERVES 6

1 onion, finely chopped

75 g (3 oz) unsalted butter

500 g (1 lb 2 oz) risotto rice

1 glass dry white wine

1.5 litres (2½ pints) vegetable
   stock, kept simmering

grated zest and juice of 2 oranges

about 150 ml (5 fl oz) vodka

sea salt and freshly milled black pepper

4 tablespoons single cream

2 tablespoons freshly grated
   Parmesan cheese

grated orange zest for serving

Method

Fry the onion and butter together until the onion is soft. Add the rice and toast the grains, then add the wine and boil quickly to evaporate the alcohol. When the wine has been absorbed into the rice, pour in the first ladleful of hot stock, stirring constantly and allowing the liquid to be absorbed before adding more. Continue to cook the rice in this way, making sure that the rice always absorbs the stock before you add more liquid. After about 15 minutes, stir in the orange zest and juice and the vodka, season to taste and continue to cook the risotto. When the risotto is creamy and velvety but the rice grains are still firm to the bite, take it off the heat and stir in the cream and Parmesan. Stir through and cover. Leave to rest for 2 minutes, then transfer to a warmed serving dish and serve sprinkled with orange zest.

White Wine Risotto
Risotto al Vino Bianco

One of the simplest, most traditional of all the risotti, it goes without saying that whatever wine is used to make the risotto should also be the wine that is drunk with it.

SERVES 4

1 onion, finely chopped

¼ celery stick, very finely chopped

75 g (3 oz) unsalted butter

400 g (14 oz) Arborio rice

½ bottle (or even a whole bottle) dry white wine such as Pinot Grigio, Gavi or Bianco di Franciacorta

1 litre (1¾ pints) chicken or vegetable stock, kept simmering

50 g (2 oz) Parmesan cheese, freshly grated

sea salt and freshly milled black pepper

Method

Fry the onion and celery very gently in half the butter until soft and translucent. Add all the rice and toast the grains, turning them in the butter and onion until opaque and crackling hot. Stir in a large glass full of white wine and stir until the alcohol has evaporated, then add more wine and repeat. When all the wine has been used up and the alcohol has been boiled off, begin to add the hot stock. Stir constantly and allow all the liquid to be absorbed before adding more. Continue to cook the rice in this way for about 20 minutes, stirring and making sure that the rice always absorbs the stock before you add more liquid. When the risotto is creamy and velvety but the rice grains are still firm to the bite, take it off the heat and stir in the remaining butter and the Parmesan. Adjust the seasoning and cover. Leave to rest for about 2 minutes, then stir once more and transfer to a warmed platter to serve.

Red Wine Risotto
Risotto al Vino Rosso

The unfortunate thing about this risotto is the way it looks when it has finished cooking: a funny purple colour! If you get used to the colour, the flavour is as fabulous as the wine you use to make it.

SERVES 4

1 red onion, chopped

$1/2$ celery stick, very finely chopped

75 g (3 oz) unsalted butter

2 fresh sage leaves, finely chopped

400 g (14 oz) risotto rice, preferably
   Vialone Nano or Arborio

$1/2$–1 bottle full-bodied red wine with
   plenty of tannin, such as Chianti,
   Barolo, Nebbiolo or Dolcetto

50 g (2 oz) Parmesan cheese,
   freshly grated

sea salt and freshly milled
   black pepper

Method

Fry the onion and celery with half the butter and the sage until the onion and celery are soft and translucent. Add the rice and stir until all the grains are toasted, opaque and crackling hot. Do not let the rice or the vegetables brown during this process. Add the first glass of red wine. Stir until the wine has been absorbed and the alcohol has evaporated, then add more wine. Continue in this way until all the wine has been used. At this point, start adding the hot stock, stirring constantly and allowing the liquid to be absorbed before adding more. Continue to cook the rice in this way for about 20 minutes, making sure that the rice always absorbs the stock before you add more liquid. When the risotto is creamy and velvety but the rice grains are still firm to the bite, take it off the heat and stir in the other half of the butter and the Parmesan. Adjust the seasoning and cover. Leave to stand for about 2 minutes, stir one last time, then transfer to a warmed platter and serve.

Barolo Risotto
Risotto al Barolo

In the Piedmont, the success of this risotto is judged by how much Barolo you can get the rice to absorb, and in order to achieve this you must keep the cooking process very slow.

Barolo is arguably the king of Italian wines. It is made in Piedmont from the Nebbiolo grape, which is also used to make other Piedmontese wines. An indication of just how special this wine is considered to be is that this is the only Piedmontese wine for which the grapes are governed by special legislation. Unlike other grape harvests in the region, the harvest for Barolo grapes has to start on the same day for all wine producers. Very high in tannin, Barolo is a full-bodied and portentous wine which, according to Italy's first Prime Minister, Cavour, is: ' good after ten years, very good after fifteen, but excellent after twenty'. In fact, the wine can last an entire century, and takes on a wonderful brick-red colour as it ages. You will discover that the wine's price reflects its quality, so this really is one risotto to save for the most special of occasions.

SERVES 6

200 g (7 oz) fresh or dried borlotti beans	1 carrot
300 g (11 oz) stewing veal or beef	1 litre (1³/₄ pints) cold water
2 onions	sea salt and freshly milled black pepper
1 celery stick	120 g (4¹/₂ oz) unsalted butter
	500 g (1 lb 2 oz) risotto rice
	2 (or even 3) bottles of good **Barolo**
	75 g (3 oz) Parmesan cheese, freshly grated

Method

First, cook the beans. If they are very fresh, simply shell them, cover with water and boil them gently for about 20–30 minutes until tender. If they are dried, they will need to be soaked thoroughly overnight, then drained, rinsed and boiled fast for 5 minutes in fresh water. Drain again, cover with water and simmer gently for 45–60 minutes until tender. In either case, do not add salt until the beans are tender as the salt will make the skins toughen. When the beans are cooked, drain them and keep to one side until required.

Next, make the stock. Put the meat into a pan with 1 onion, the celery and the carrot. Cover with the cold water, add a little salt and bring to the boil. Simmer gently for about 2 hours. Remove the meat and the vegetables from the stock pot, trim the meat and chop both the meat and the vegetables finely. Reserve these and strain the stock. Adjust the seasoning if necessary and keep the stock hot until required.

Now melt half the butter in a large, heavy-based pan. Chop the second onion finely and fry it in the butter until soft and golden. Add all the rice and toast it quickly in the hot butter and onion. When it is coated in butter, shiny and hot, add the first glass full of Barolo. Stir and allow the alcohol to evaporate, then add a ladleful of hot stock, stir and allow the rice to absorb the liquid, then add more Barolo. Continue in this way, adding wine and stock alternately and stirring in between each addition, until the rice is half cooked. This should take about 10 minutes. Add salt and pepper to taste. Then add the beans and add more wine and stock. Cook for a further 4 minutes, then add the chopped meat and vegetables. Continue as before until the risotto is creamy and velvety but the rice grains are still firm to the bite. Remove from the heat and add the rest of the butter and all the Parmesan. Stir together very thoroughly, then cover with a lid and leave to stand for about 5 minutes before turning out on to a warmed serving platter. Take it to the table at once.

Sweet Risotto Cake
Torta di Riso Dolce

A very eggy, delicious cake with the rice holding it all together. If you wanted to, you could add a few chopped nuts, raisins, sultanas, pine nuts, or candied fruits as we have done for the cake in the photograph.

MAKES ONE 25 CM (10 IN) CAKE

150 g (5 oz) short-grain risotto rice

1.25 litres (2¼ pints) milk

butter for greasing

2 tablespoons semolina

8 eggs

250 g (9 oz) caster sugar

3 tablespoons brandy

grated zest or juice of ½ lemon

Method

Put the rice and about two-thirds of the milk into a pan. Bring to the boil, simmer for 10 minutes, then drain.

Preheat the oven to 180°C/350°F/gas mark 4. Butter a deep 25 cm (10 in) cake tin thoroughly, then sprinkle with the semolina. Do not use a loose-bottomed tin or all the liquid will ooze away. Turn the cake tin upside-down to remove any loose semolina.

Beat the eggs in a large bowl until foaming and pale yellow. Add the sugar gradually, beating constantly, then add the brandy and the lemon zest or juice. Stir thoroughly, then add the rice and all the remaining milk. Pour into the cake tin. Bake for about 50 minutes or until a wooden skewer inserted in the centre comes out clean. The cake should be well set and golden brown. Serve warm or cold.

Champagne Risotto
Risotto allo Champagne

This is probably the most difficult of all the risotti to make properly because the art lies in keeping a little of the fizz in the Champagne coming through into the rest of the textures in the dish. You must be careful to use a stock that will not overpower the taste of the wine you are using, and that you don't rest the risotto for too long at the end, otherwise you will lose all the sparkle.

SERVES 4

2 small shallots, very finely chopped

1/4 celery stick, very finely chopped

75 g (3 oz) unsalted butter

400 g (14 oz) risotto rice, preferably Carnaroli

3/4–1 bottle Champagne or sparkling wine or Prosecco

1.25 litres (2 1/4 pints) light chicken or vegetable stock

50 g (2 oz) Parmesan cheese, freshly grated

sea salt and freshly milled black pepper

Method

Fry the shallots and celery very gently in half the butter until soft and translucent. Add all the rice and toast the grains, turning them in the butter and onion until toasted and shiny. Pour out one glass of the Champagne or wine and set it aside to use at the very end of the cooking time. Stir a large glass of Champagne or wine into the pan and stir until the alcohol has evaporated, then add more wine and repeat. When all the Champagne or wine has been used up (except the reserved glass), begin to add the hot stock. Stir constantly and allow all the liquid to be absorbed before adding more. Continue to cook the rice in this way, stirring and making sure that the rice always absorbs the stock before you add more liquid. After about 20 minutes, when the risotto is creamy and velvety but the rice grains are still firm to the bite, take it off the heat and stir in the remaining butter and the Parmesan. Adjust the seasoning and stir in the reserved glass of Champagne or wine. Cover and leave to rest for 1 minute, then stir once more and transfer to a warmed platter to serve.

Sweet Chocolate Rice
Riso Dolce al Cioccolato

As children, we often enjoyed *riso al latte* for our supper, which is simply risotto rice simmered in milk until soft, then sweetened with a little sugar before eating. Here is a slightly more elegant and delicious version, using the very best cooking chocolate. You can add nuts and candied fruits if you like.

SERVES 4

400 g (14 oz) risotto rice

1.2 litres (2 pints) full-fat milk

a tiny pinch of ground cinnamon

3 tablespoons caster sugar

grated zest of $1/2$ orange

100 g (4 oz) cooking
chocolate, melted

2 tablespoons double cream,
plus extra for serving

Method

Put the rice into a pan and pour over the milk. Bring to the boil, then simmer very gently for about 20 minutes until the rice is tender. Remove from the heat and stir in the cinnamon, sugar, orange zest and chocolate. Cover and rest for about 2 minutes, then stir in the cream and transfer to individual bowls to serve. Serve warm, not piping hot and offer extra cream if you like.

Maxine's Ice-cream Risotto
Gelato di Risotto

This recipe was created by a very good friend and colleague, Maxine Clarke, whose name I am delighted to mention in this book! A superb creamy vanilla ice-cream with a barely perceptible granular texture, it seems to have originated in Sicily, famed for its ice-cream, but is now popular all over Italy. In Sicily, rose water, cinnamon and even ginger are used as flavourings. Fresh peaches or figs both go perfectly with the ice-cream, as you can see in the photograph.

SERVES 8

120 g (4½ oz) risotto rice,
   preferably Vialone Nano
600 ml (1 pint) creamy milk
1 vanilla pod, split

175 g (6 oz) caster sugar
600 ml (1 pint) double cream, chilled
1 tablespoon orange flower water
  or rose water

Method

Preheat the oven to 180°C/350°F/gas mark 4. Put the rice, milk and vanilla pod in a flameproof casserole and bring to the boil. Remove from the heat, cover tightly, then cook in the oven for about 1 hour until the rice is very tender. Alternatively, simmer gently on top of the stove for at least 25 minutes, stirring constantly, until very soft.

Remove from the oven, discard the vanilla pod and stir in the sugar. Cover the surface with greaseproof paper, leave to cool, then chill in the fridge for at least 1 hour.

Stir in the cream and orange flower water or rose water. Freeze in an ice-cream maker according to the manufacturer's instructions until the ice-cream has the consistency of whipped cream. Transfer to a freezer container and freeze for at least 2 hours. If you do not have an ice-cream maker, place in a freezer container in the freezer, then remove and whisk the ice-cream every 30 minutes or so during freezing to break down the ice crystals and ensure a smooth-textured result. Transfer to the fridge to soften before serving.

Index